MW00800250

STERNBERG AND DIETRICH

Sternberg and Dietrich

THE PHENOMENOLOGY OF SPECTACLE

James Phillips

OXFORD

UNIVERSITY PRESS

OXFORD
UNIVERSITY PRESS

Oxford University Press is a department of the University of Oxford. It furthers
the University's objective of excellence in research, scholarship, and education
by publishing worldwide. Oxford is a registered trade mark of Oxford University
Press in the UK and certain other countries.

Published in the United States of America by Oxford University Press
198 Madison Avenue, New York, NY 10016, United States of America.

© Oxford University Press 2019

Library of Congress Cataloging-in-Publication Data
Names: Phillips, James, 1970– author.
Title: Sternberg and Dietrich : the phenomenology of spectacle / James Phillips.
Description: New York City : Oxford University Press, 2019. |
Includes bibliographical references and index.
Identifiers: LCCN 2018019850 (print) | LCCN 2018021766 (ebook) |
ISBN 9780190915254 (updf) | ISBN 9780190915261 (epub) |
ISBN 9780190915247 (cloth : alk. paper)
Subjects: LCSH: Von Sternberg, Josef, 1894–1969—Criticism and interpretation. |
Dietrich, Marlene—Criticism and interpretation. Classification: LCC PN1998.3.V66 (ebook) |
LCC PN1998.3.V66 P55 2018 (print) | DDC 791.4302/33092—dc23
LC record available at https://lccn.loc.gov/2018019850

9 8 7 6 5 4 3 2

Printed by Sheridan Books, Inc., United States of America

To Peter Brennan and his genius for happiness

Contents

Introduction: Dietrich's Face and the Talking Picture 1

1. Shanghai Express: Making Room for Faith in Appearances 23

2. Blonde Venus: A Sale of Two Bodies 41

3. The Scarlet Empress: History as Farce 59

4. The Devil Is a Woman: Against the Off-Screen 75

Conclusion: Toward an Ethics of the Moving Image 91

NOTES 105
REFERENCES 117
INDEX 121

Introduction
DIETRICH'S FACE AND THE TALKING PICTURE

IN THE SEVEN sound films that Josef von Sternberg made with Marlene Dietrich between 1930 and 1935, the face of his star, in assuming the form in which it was to become famous, exploits the unexpected possibilities and licenses with which synchronization confronted the cinema. It is the face that knows how to enjoy its freedom from the easy legibility that the silent film demanded of actors for the purpose of carrying the narrative. The close-up, having ceased to preoccupy itself with registering reactions, can give itself up to the scrutiny of a woman's deliberation of prospects and proposals. There is no need to rush; there is no desire to rush. This is not—or not simply—a director's infatuation with his star. In the Sternberg close-up, the face has withdrawn from its immediate surroundings and takes the time to think. Mulling over its options, knowing that there are plenty of other sign-systems at work in the synchronized film to advance the story, the face acquires and inhabits an agency and spontaneity specific to it. If Marlene appears to resist objectification in Sternberg's films, if no gaze can confidently pretend to reify her, it is because her face looks out upon a future that is irreducible to the determinate situations in which she finds herself. It is the face as subject. Hers is a face whose affective volatility is cued to the cracks in the present. At issue is not the aloofness with which Garbo already had looked beyond the environments that constrained her, just as the alternatives Marlene contemplates have little to do with the resolutely abstract future that can only ever be a source of melancholy. This spatiotemporal independence of Marlene's face, even as it lends itself to the publicity shots with which Paramount flooded the print media, is originally and maximally a spatiotemporal independence that Sternberg invents within the motion picture rather than from it. It is the depth that he opens up within the cinematic image by dint of mercurial changes in facial expressions deploying themselves over a white surface.

It is well known that Sternberg did not, strictly speaking, discover Dietrich when he cast her in the role of Lola Lola in *The Blue Angel* (1930). In a sense, however, Dietrich could not be discovered in the numerous silent films in which she had been playing bit parts since 1923. She had to lie in wait for the sound film and for how Sternberg might find a way of shooting her to suit it. Much has long been made of the celebrated butterfly lighting whereby Sternberg and his cinematographer Lee Garmes illuminated for all the world to see a beauty that Dietrich had until then not known better than to keep hidden in broad daylight. Yet there is in Marlene's beauty also something inseparable from the constellation of challenges and opportunities of the sound film. It does not so much preexist the sound film, a potentiality captive to poor lighting and the weight that Sternberg was to insist that Dietrich lose, as come into being with the sound film's greater tolerance for emotional inscrutability. Marlene's is the face of the talking picture in its break with the cosmopolitan communication that had conscripted for its medium the physiognomies and gestures of the actors of the silent film.

In *Der sichtbare Mensch* (1924), Béla Balázs reflects on this affective internationalism of the silent film with which Dietrich's peculiar talents for ambivalence are hard to reconcile:

> The laws of the film market permit only universally comprehensible facial expressions and gestures, every nuance of which is understood by princess and working girl alike from San Francisco to Smyrna. We now already have a situation in which the film speaks the only universal, common world language understood by all. Ethnic peculiarities, national specificities sometimes can lend style and colour to a film, but can never become factors in causing the story to move on, because the gestures which convey the meaning and decide the course of the action must be uniformly comprehensible to every audience everywhere, otherwise the producer will lose money on the film.[1]

If Chaplin was able to dispense with intertitles in his silent films because of the extreme clarity of his actions and expressions, Dietrich by contrast was able to linger within the uncertain intersections and crossovers of the emotions because the narrative burden had been assumed by the recorded dialogue. She brings into play an independence that resembles but differs in kind from the surliness with which Georgia Hale, Evelyn Brent, and Betty Compson respond to their surroundings in Sternberg's earlier work. Whereas the stories of the silent films in which they appear are stories told by their faces of how their initial suspicions are mollified, Dietrich never lets herself be won over by the story being told around her. Hers is the face that emerged into view when the dust settled on the ruins of the Tower of Babel of the silent film—her features compose the letters of the judgment on the latter's aspirations. While Balázs entertained hopes that the sound film, after an initial flirtation with dialogue, would apply itself to recovering what the silent film had accomplished by way of a universal gesturology, Sternberg and Dietrich were to embark for a different destination. Opting for neither the photographed theater that Balázs considered the sound film's regression to the earliest efforts of the cinema nor the corporeal cosmopolitanism by virtue of which he believed the silent film came into its own as an art, they undertake to construct a new type of image. Together Sternberg and Dietrich will reinvent light, investing it with a milkiness that is at once transparent and opaque. The luminous and limpid cloud of their films is the native element of Dietrich's stardom, for she is there in plain sight with the double conspicuousness of beauty and fame while also unplaceably exotic and inassimilable to the concerns and cognitive habits of the notional everyman. The eye sees, but it also can never be done with looking, because something is withheld from it without, however, being imperceptible. This archness is inherent in all beauty and merges with and leavens the archness of Dietrich's own persona.

Not having to ward off the viewer who cannot enter the frame, Marlene is profligate with invitations. But she invites without letting the consciousness of her invitation disappear behind her sheer physical presence. By means of this consciousness and agency of the address, Sternberg and Dietrich imbue the proximity and intimacy of the close-up with a simultaneous distance. The close-up suffers a defeat in the epistemological claims made for it, because an increase in visibility does not here stand in correlation with an increase in intelligibility. This should not be confused with a decadent aestheticism, let alone a cognitive nihilism. What Sternberg and Dietrich contrive to produce—and what tests their fortitude, ingenuity, and combined technical and histrionic talents—is a close-up of a human face. This cannot be taken for granted based on the automatism of cinematographic recording, because the defining difference of the human face from objects is an affair of ethics and not of technology.

The obsessive attention to detail with which Sternberg and Dietrich went about the close-up has, of course, less to do with responding directly to a long-standing ethical imperative than with converting this imperative into an artistic challenge.

Human personhood in its very irreducibility to phenomena and to the various protocols for their use was to be rendered phenomenally: the noumenal was to be made flesh. To censure Sternberg for not treating every face in his films the way he treats Marlene's is to interpret ethically the conversion of an ethical imperative into an artistic challenge. This would be a category mistake. The artistic challenge is a response to the ethical imperative and is not a substitute for it (needless to say, a face does not become the site of an ethical demand only when the full resources of a major Hollywood studio are at its disposal). Where there is a fault in relation to this ethical imperative, a fault that corresponds to the sin of idolatry, it lies with the viewer who, unable or unwilling to see past beauty and fame, reserves for the star the comportment that is due to all persons as human beings. Sternberg himself, admittedly, dallies with this fault. He commits it artistically and as such he does not commit it in earnest. Within the cinematic horizon of spectacle he cannot but adhere to the limitations of the phenomenal, even as he puts them into question. Marlene is the subject that has come down to earth to dwell among the objects of perception. She relieves the viewer of the ethical imperative to look beyond the thingliness of that which presents itself to the gaze because she offers a tangible equivalent of that beyond. This is something other than the infernal temptation of pure materiality. For those who have only eyes to see it is even a training in a sensitivity to the non-givenness of the human person. In the dark, where we cease to show ourselves as an object among objects, we are all what Marlene is in the light.

A visual rendition of transcendental personhood is intrinsically ambiguous. It points to a beyond of the phenomenal realm, indicating the deficiencies and moral shortcomings of a practice whose assumption is that it deals only ever with objects—in the case of Sternberg's collaborations with Dietrich, this takes the shape specifically of an assertion of female agency. And yet, the beyond to which it ostensibly and ostentatiously points is itself but a fold within the visual—the face is less the outward expression of a person than a surface that has confected its own version of subjectivity. The paradox of their collaboration is that Sternberg instrumentalized Dietrich's face to create a suggestion or appearance of agency. Given that the expressiveness of an actor's face is not reliably at the beck and call of psychological movements within the depth of the character, Sternberg did not always deem it advisable to discuss with Dietrich her characters' motivations. When it came time to shoot her final close-up in *Morocco* (1930), for instance, he directed her to count backwards from forty, subsequently passing off the visible evidence of her mental concentration on this task for the internal debate over whether to follow Legionnaire Tom Brown (Gary Cooper) out over the dunes.[2]

In his reflections on screen acting in his autobiography, *Fun in a Chinese Laundry* (1965), Sternberg does not disparage the intelligence and autonomy of actors simply to exalt his own. The nature of studio shooting is such that the intelligence that would preside internally over the production of meaningful gestures and expressions is confounded:

> Children, animals, or actors are deliberately invested with an intelligence that seems to stem from them. In the popular film cartoons the audience knows that behind the tail-wagging duck there is someone who is causing it to move and squawk; and when a ventriloquist pulls a puppet out of a box, the source of the doll's intelligence is understood not to be his own. But when a film actor who undergoes considerably more manipulation than any duck or dummy begins to appear to function, he is judged, even by the shrewdest critic, on the basis of being a self-determining and self-contained unit of intelligence. This is not so. The machinery of the motion picture does not permit it. [. . .] In contrast to the theatre, the actor who ventures into the films not only will not know where the audience is but he will soon cease to care whether there is one or not. Three cameras may be aimed to him from as many directions. A camera may be pointed at him from ten feet above his head and another from below his feet, and he may or may not know what part of his person will be visible afterward unless he is in constant contact with the cameraman who, having troubles of his own, may have come to the sound conclusion that it is none of the actor's business. The actor himself cannot judge what part of himself is being immortalized as it is not his distance from the camera but the focal length of the lens which determines this.[3]

According to Sternberg, the multiple disorientations of the studio set press upon actors a choice: either to acknowledge the loss of significative agency and to entrust themselves to the formative impulses of the director or to persist in a baseless fantasy of control, thereby achieving nothing besides wreaking havoc on the production. Dietrich, in contrast to her industry peers, acceded to Sternberg's demands with a passivity that conjured up its own inordinate self-discipline: "No puppet in the history of the world has been submitted to as much manipulation as a leading lady of mine who, in seven films, not only had hinges and voice under a control other than her own but the expression of her eyes and the nature of her thoughts."[4] Dietrich endured what other actors were unwilling to endure because she was committed to the image that Sternberg was fashioning of her in the furnace of Paramount's studio lighting: "In my films Marlene is not herself. Remember that, Marlene is not Marlene. I am Marlene, she knows that better than anyone."[5] The complement of this declaration of directorial authority, however, is that we cannot see Sternberg properly in the standard portrait photograph—just as we are exhorted here to discern his features overlaid on Marlene's face, we should also overlay his face with her features if we are to see it at all.

This perversity at the heart of Marlene's cinematic autonomy is alluded to in Rainer Werner Fassbinder's *The Bitter Tears of Petra von Kant* (1972). The character called Marlene (Irm Hermann) has no text to speak and is bullied and exploited by Petra (Margit Carstensen) who palms off her designs as her own work. When in the final scene, having begun to rally from the emotional upheaval of her failed romance with Karin Thimm (Hanna Schygulla), Petra proposes henceforth to recognize Marlene as a person and a collaborator, this prompts Marlene to pack her suitcase—it is recognition that constitutes the last straw, for measured by the terms of their relationship it is abuse and estrangement. In leaving, Marlene does not so much rediscover her autonomy after years of servitude and self-effacement as uphold an autonomy that can accommodate, even relish mistreatment but draws the line at recognition. To be Marlene is to be a zone of undecidability between agency and passivity.

Unlike Fassbinder's Marlene, Sternberg's does speak. And unlike the younger Garbo, she was not already established as a European star in Hollywood before the arrival of the sound film (at least in a commercially viable form): she did not have

FIGURE 1.1. Marlene Dietrich as Shanghai Lily in *Shanghai Express* (dir. Josef von Sternberg, Paramount Pictures, 1932).

FIGURE I.2. Irm Hermann as Marlene in *The Bitter Tears of Petra von Kant* (dir. Rainer Werner Fassbinder, Tango Film, 1972).

to ask the public to adjust its understanding of her to make room for her accented speaking voice. The voice is crucial to the construction of her image and to the crystallization of her fame. It is not a voice that can be satisfactorily classified as German, as though all that one needed to know of it and to make of it were comprised in the stereotypes and predictabilities associated with Germanness.[6] Dietrich's voice does not immerse itself in the conformity of any given community of language-users. When she first sings in *Morocco*, the film that introduced her to audiences in the United States, she sings in French. If one were to appraise the performance solely by the criteria whose normal object is the song production of an operatic soprano or Broadway belter, then the nightclub's rapturous reception of her interpretation of "Quand l'amour meurt" will necessarily be puzzling, inviting comparisons with the mice's enthusiasm for the sonically unremarkable piping of Kafka's Josephine. The voice is by no means irrelevant to the performance, but it must be evaluated in conjunction with its visual counterpoint. More a *diseuse* than a singer, Dietrich does not allow the audience to become absorbed in the lushness and technical mastery of a human voice. Setting up residence on the threshold between speaking and singing, she participates in the musicalization of the everyday. Georges Millandy's lyrics for "Quand l'amour meurt," for the audience member who does not know French, become the white noise in which she moves (for its part, what intelligibility there is to the garglingly delivered lyrics with their seasonal observations on the passing of love does not extend to a commentary on the film's narrative). The song is one component among others in an extraordinary performance of everydayness. That Dietrich does not burst into song but rather recites the verses is in keeping with an artistic reimagining of the casual.

The scene begins with Dietrich in her dressing room, fixing her hair with the aid of a hand mirror and going over the opening verses of "Quand l'amour meurt." She toys momentarily with a fan, amused at the thought that she could need it to keep her cool in the African heat. When with an enormous hoop earring in his right ear the flustered impresario Lo Tinto (Paul Porcasi) arrives and tells her the house is packed, she calmly smokes a cigarette and pops her top hat, wordlessly half-attending to his advice to find a protector among the officers of the Foreign Legion. Lo Tinto mops his brow with a crumpled handkerchief and with neither an entreaty nor a demand Dietrich has him help her into her black dinner jacket. The supreme self-possession she exhibits she then carries with her out onto the nightclub stage. It is a self-possession whose basis is a serene good humor rather than intransigence. It comes across even as a kind of antihistrionic self-possession, for the passage over the threshold separating the dressing room from the stage does not coincide with the adoption of a different personality tailored to the satisfaction of an audience's expectations. The impresario, having fallen down to mocking laughter as he pulls at the curtain to open it, pleads with his customers to welcome his new act with their "usual discriminating kindness." This is wishful thinking, as Monsieur La Bessière (Adolphe Menjou) explains to a neighbor since the clientele is wont to greet newcomers "rather unpleasantly." Dietrich's entry is duly met with howls of odium from the socially and ethnically diverse audience (that this is in response *solely* to the provocation of her cross-dressing is a reading of the scene that must be discounted in the light of what we have just learned regarding this public's reception habits). His eyes narrowing, and his lips pursed in acrimonious suspicion, Gary Cooper sits in the front row of tables. Dietrich is altogether unfazed and takes her time before commencing her number. She will be neither hurried nor harried. Tellingly she does not begin the song at the beginning: it is as though what she had already sung to herself in the privacy of her dressing room is to count toward the performance, since what she is performing is her own everydayness in a normalization of cross-dressing and lesbian flirtation.

Dietrich's nonchalance toward the public in Lo Tinto's cabaret is, as it were, facilitated by the public that she addresses via the camera. This is her true audience just as the seething expressionism of bodies around her is in essence part of her act, given that her composure is underscored by the juxtaposition. His hair disheveled, his collar undone, the shirt-sleeved conductor of the band must yield to Marlene's visual claim to be the one actually in charge of the scene. She knows that she will win her fellow performers over, that their overblown belligerence will metamorphose into enchantment. And whatever vociferous condemnation of cross-dressing there was at the outset, eclipsing anything that a sane moviegoer might be inclined to vent in the very different social space of a cinema, vanishes without a trace (aware that the projection on the screen has of its own no eyes to see and no ears to hear, the viewer who is induced to delegate to the on-screen audience the manifestation of his or her own outrage at this scrambling of the socially acceptable modes of gender display will be let down). Dietrich looks less past the physical audience in front of her than not as far as it. There are gestures and facial expressions in her performance that are too subtle to make much of an impression on audience members seated at any distance from the stage and having to make sense of proceedings through clouds of cigarette smoke, the flicker of fans, and the bobbing intervening masses of unruly spectators. The close-up is the measure to which at these points Dietrich cuts her routine. And assessed purely as an object of visual perception, the microphone that someone with Dietrich's meagre vocal projection would require in order to be heard in a venue of that size is sacrificed to the priorities and possibilities of the close-up.

FIGURE I.3. Marlene Dietrich as Amy Jolly performing gender for herself alone in Lo Tinto's nightclub in *Morocco* (dir. Josef von Sternberg, Paramount Pictures, 1930).

For all the brilliance and charm of the scene as played by Dietrich and directed by Sternberg, it arguably works against the psychological coherence of the narrative trajectory of Dietrich's character, Amy Jolly. The poise with which she comports herself on the stage has been too firmly entrenched for the reckless abandon of the film's ending not to seem a leap too far: the performance of "Quand l'amour meurt" with its same-sex kiss refuses to surrender its independence from the overarching storyline of Amy Jolly's passion for Gary Cooper's Tom Brown.[7] Psychological realism, concerned as it is with characterization integrated over the length of a film, is, however, hostile territory for a star, because it asks the star to submerge his or her persona in a role that can have no life beyond the movie in question. Structurally, Sternberg's collaborations with Dietrich at Paramount are exercises in the construction of an environment in which a star can flourish. There is a jaggedness to the montage that allows individual scenes and shots to hum with an intractable vitality. Sternberg is a notable counterexample to the oft-repeated claim that classical Hollywood subordinates everything to the narrative. The unmotivated is regularly given its head in Sternberg's films: inasmuch as it is an ally of Dietrich's transcendence as a star, puncturing the semantic holism with which a narrative threatens to consume its setting, it is not a thoughtless caprice. An instance of this disruptive practice is the Ozu-like shot of the two dolls that Sternberg interleaves in the cabaret sequence in *Morocco* between the establishing shots of the waiting audience and the scene in Amy Jolly's dressing room. This is not the planting of a clue. Although the two dolls—one a gift from Sternberg to Dietrich—later figure among the jumble of items in Amy Jolly's bedroom, the whimsicality of the shot is not subsequently recuperated by the narrative. Besides putting an abrupt stop to the frenzied movement of the establishing shots of the audience and thereby granting to Marlene's movements in the dressing room the freedom to lay claim to their own momentum, to begin from scratch under their own steam, this shot of the dolls is a nod to the disjointed, disparate nature of the everyday in its difference from the organicism of narrative.[8]

Dietrich, leaving her dressing room for the stage, remains in the openness of the everyday. She strolls the nightclub floor as though it were a public space, a promenade where a gentleman might at his leisure but not without invitation kiss a female passerby. The double hesitation that precedes Dietrich's kiss differentiates it from the prerogative of a stage performer who, with an eye to an effect on the room as a whole, takes advantage of the physical passivity of an audience member. Dietrich's double hesitation transports the kiss from the theatrical to the everyday: it is an act whose *ratio finalis* does not lie in the gaze of third parties.[9]

Although Laura Mulvey refers to the image of Dietrich in *Morocco* in her examination of the male gaze in cinema, she does not analyze its most famous scene.

Mulvey's description does not tally: "The beauty of the woman as object and the screen space coalesce; she is no longer the bearer of guilt but a perfect product, whose body, stylized and fragmented by close-ups, is the content of the film and the direct recipient of the spectator's look."[10] Objectification does not capture what is at stake in Sternberg's solicitude for the pictorial space enclosed by the frame to the detriment of the narrative. Dietrich does not win her independence from the narrative only to surrender as an object to the gaze of the heterosexual male viewer. In her independence, she returns the spectator's look.[11]

One of the achievements of the close-up in Dietrich's films with Sternberg is this disruption of the spectator's voyeuristic impunity. For it to be plausible at all that a projection on a screen has the agency to look back at the spectator in the cinema auditorium, the expression on Dietrich's face and in her eyes does not only have to affirm a degree of self-sufficiency in relation to the scene (any bad actor not committed to his or her role will carry this off), but it also has to be readable as applying to the spectator's own independence from the narrative. The polymorphous affectivity of Dietrich's face is a Rorschach inkblot in which viewers can believe they discern what is pertinent privately to them. One also might compare Dietrich's face to a Noh mask whose expression varies depending on the angle at which it is held and from which it is seen—what are spatial differences in perspective in the case of the mask are, in the case of Marlene, differences among the viewers' moods, expectations, and histories. The genesis of the cinematic face that looks back remedies one of the scandals of the moving image. Whereas Hegel had spoken of the work of art as "a thousand-eyed Argus" from whose every aspect and surface "the inner soul and spirit" looks out, a century later the moving image was to adopt the opposite course, managing to make the human eye itself into a mere thing among things.[12] If within the physical space that they share as bodies the actor on stage in a theater is able to look a given spectator in the eye, Dietrich's peculiar talent and accomplishment in her films with Sternberg is to appear to do the same from a screen even after her death.

The emphasis in film studies on the moviegoer's gaze is, to an extent, an understandable corollary of the marginalizing of his or her bodily movement in the determination of vantage point. If the moviegoer can be defined by the condition of gazing at a screen, it is because the director, monopolizing the power to maneuver within the space of the shot, loosens the moviegoer's bond between sight and motor skills. One is all the more someone who simply gazes, the less one's gaze is tied up with the movements by means of which one wends one's way among the obstacles of concrete space. Theories of the agency of the gaze compensate, as it were, for the incapacitation of the moviegoer's body with respect to the spatiality of the cinematic image. There is a contraction of the horizon of agency when the sensorimotor nexus of the gaze becomes the preserve of the filmmaker, when it is the director who decides, for instance, just how much of a ceiling we get to see in an indoor sequence, whose re-action to a revelation we will inspect and whether to elide the distances between settings that the characters must travel. The idea of the domineering gaze of the mov-iegoer is a restorative fantasy inasmuch as it makes light of the passivity that the film-maker instills by moving in our place. This is not to deny that there are also cogent reasons for acknowledging the genuine oppressiveness of the objectifying gaze or that the agency of this gaze is in any way innocuous for having a basis in fantasy. If we think it fit to accept the filmmaker's offer to provide us with an extra set of eyes, a set of disembodied eyes with which we might look on scenes without being physically present, and hence without fear of immediate retaliation or reproof from participants who would otherwise be affronted by the brazenness of our gaze, what we gain from this seeming instrumentalization of the filmmaker's vision has to be weighed against what we lose in terms of the integration of sight with our own movements.

This interruption of the sensorimotor nexus consigns the moviegoer to spectacle, severely qualifying the cinema's pretensions to realism. Provided the camera is mo-bile, provided there is more than the one shot in the film, the long take extolled by André Bazin is not enough to pull the moviegoer back from the clutches of cine-matic spectacle. Unable to restore the moviegoer's everyday experience of the senso-rimotor nexus, whatever reality effect the long take can be said to bring off does not break the spell of spectatorship: the lived reality of a moving body in concrete space is not retrieved. Sternberg, who is pointedly not a director of the long take, nourishes and reinforces the cinema's ingrained tendencies to spectacle. He takes hold of the viewer's perception and, pinning it to his own sensorimotor nexus, absconds with it. The business of the viewer is to look.

The gaze, in being momentarily released from its dependence on the movements of the body, embarks on a sort of holiday from the ethical questions that attend human agency. It sets out to absolve itself unilaterally of ethical responsibility, telling itself that it cannot count as an agent because it does nothing but passively take in what is presented to it. This, at least, is the conception of the gaze that feminist film criticism has sought to debunk, alleging that cinematic spectacle is far less a holiday from ethical demands than a training in the objectification of women that is then applied to flesh-and-blood human beings away from the act of cinematic spectatorship. An assumption here is that cinematic fictions acquire their ethical pertinence only when considered in relation to the larger world in which the sen-sorimotor nexus reasserts itself. The ethical evaluation of the gaze concerns the atti-tude toward that which is depicted rather than toward the image as such: Sternberg, who makes a spectacle out of Dietrich, is decried for what his images say about his attitude toward their referent. But in not asking the viewer to look beyond the image to a referent separate from it, in coaxing from spectacle all of its gifts for self-sufficiency, Sternberg can be found to be morally at fault only by an ethics that does not accept that attitudes toward the image *as image* can be ethical. He is a moralist of images even as he converts the ethical imperative of the human face into an artistic challenge. Sternberg's Dietrich is autonomy as image. The moral proof of our attitude toward the image does not lie in our subsequent dealings with its referent: it lies in our preparedness to acknowledge autonomy in the image itself. If it is crucial to Dietrich's autonomy that she returns the viewer's gaze, it is no less crucial to the autonomy of the image that the viewer's sensorimotor nexus snap asunder.

The image comes into a life of its own with this chastening of the subject's sense of his or her own agency. It runs rampant in the space that the moviegoer is only ever able to view from outside. Jean Mitry draws attention to the novelty of the cinema on the score of the perception of space: "whereas space in the theater never changes, in the cinema each shot involves *its own* representation, that is, the point of view and *specific dimension* created by the relationships between the represented space and the invariable frame lines."[13] There is a continuity between the space on the theatrical stage and the space in the auditorium that does not exist between the space in the shot and the space in which the moviegoer sits. A change in position within the auditorium will have an impact on what is visible on stage: opera glasses aside, if one wishes to see something on stage at close range, one has to and can move forward. Even if this agency of the body in determining the field of vision and its contents is seldom exercised in the theater (the general practice is to remain in one's seat), the theatrical presentation does not emancipate the eye from the body's position in the way that the cinematic image does. Without moving his or her head either up or down, left or right, the moviegoer perceives the objects on screen and the space in which they are filmed now from one angle, now from another, now in a long shot, now in close-up, now in a tracking shot, now in freeze-frame. Sight drifts from the body's control. One can always stand up and leave the cinema auditorium, thereby restoring the sensorimotor feedback by means of which we navigate concrete space. But so long as one persists in watching the film, one's gaze is not fully one's own. The gaze that objectifies the figures on screen also in effect paralyzes the bodies it invades in the auditorium—to watch a film is to render one's gaze a hostage to the movements of a camera one does not see.

To the distinction that Mitry draws between theater and cinema can be conjoined a further distinction between static depictions of three-dimensional space and cinema. A photograph or a drawing that exploits geometrical perspective differs from a theatrical presentation by confronting the viewer with a different space from the one he or she occupies: in examining a photograph or such a drawing we meet within the frame not only with specific objects, but also with a specific spatiality.

A painting of an object-laden indoor space—say, Vincent van Gogh's *The Night Café* (1888)—is not of a piece with the space from within which we view it (we cannot make its floor, ceiling, and walls all align *at the same time* with the floor, ceiling, and walls of whatever room we happen to be in when contemplating the work). Whereas the action on a stage is an object that we perceive within a shared space, what we perceive in *The Night Café* is van Gogh's perception of a set of objects within a space that is closed to us. Even as the graphic arts, in their cultivation of perspective, pursue the multiplication of space, thereby resembling the cinematic image, they leave intact the human body's sensorimotor nexus. The static quality of their depictions of other spaces means that any change in the dimensions of the space we are viewing is attributable to movements that we ourselves execute (we turn to look at the next picture in the gallery). In this respect, computer games and virtual reality (VR) technology constitute a retreat from the specific difference attained by the cinematic moving image with its experience of spatiality. The spaces that these later inventions open up can be markedly alien in comparison to the space occupied by the body holding a handset or wearing a headset, but by giving the user the means to decide upon a direction and upon a perspective within the illusionistic depiction of space, computer games and VR technology repair the sensorimotor nexus that the cinematic image had disabled—the new approach that cinema had initiated with respect to the body's experience of the act of perception is not pursued.

In its handling of the perception of space, the moving image induces a peculiar sensation of floating. We float because we have capitulated to another's perception of moving through space while being spared its attendant "costs" in friction and muscular exertion. As though protective of the cinema's phenomenological distinctness with respect to its circumscription of agency, Freudian psychoanalysis can but pour cold water on the popular analogy between watching a film and dreaming: the interpretation of dreams excavates within the self an agency in the selection and formation of images that in film belongs to another (the dreamer relies on repression in order to pretend to have had no say in the construction of the images he or she watches).

What we see of Marlene in *Morocco* and other films is Sternberg's perception of Marlene. It is his gaze that we see just as it is to his sensorimotor nexus that we are captive. More precisely, it is the artistic reconstruction of his gaze that we see: it is his perception not in any alleged immediacy of his sensory apparatus, but as technological commodity. In objectifying his own gaze, Sternberg endeavors as a counterbalance to subjectify the very appearance of Marlene. Her appearance of agency puckers the objectification to which he commits his own perception, redeeming it from mere thingliness. If it is at all credible that Sternberg is more Marlene than Marlene herself, it is because her image in the films he directed is his own agency as image, his own capacity to perceive reconfigured as a content of perception. If Marlene is Sternberg, the exact nature of the relationship between Sternberg and Marlene and the various male Sternberg proxies in the films, identifiable as such by the shared empirical traits of a moustache, a bearing, and a style of dress, is an open question (that Sternberg would have recourse to the "battle of the sexes" in order to stage some inner drama—to consider one answer to this question—seems absurdly narcissistic).

Sternberg's is a cinema of perception. It not only thematizes perception and builds narratives around the problems of (mis)perception, but it also shows itself prepared to abandon these very narratives in favor of the purity of its adventures in perception. The image of Dietrich exemplifies but does not exhaust this aspect of Sternberg's filmmaking. His assiduity in the forging of her star persona has its place in a larger practice in relation to storytelling. Dietrich, who was by no means a bad actor, accomplishes in her own way what Sternberg on occasion pulled off through the casting of bad actors. In one of the early attempts to rehabilitate Sternberg's reputation as a director, the underground filmmaker Jack Smith asserts the extranarrative significance of the bad actor:

A bad actor is a rich, unique, idiosyncratic, revealing of himself not of the bad script. Select the right bad actor and you can have a visual revelation very appropriate to the complex of ideas and sets of qualities that make up your film. V. S. knew this and used bad acting regularly as a technique for visual revelation (not story telling).[14]

Not every bad actor is the "right" bad actor: *Crime and Punishment* (1935), which Sternberg made on assignment at Columbia Pictures after having been forced out at Paramount, is a cautionary tale about the importance of casting. The bad actor, right or otherwise, is the uncanny double of the star. As neither disappears into the role, they both foreground the immediate phenomenality of what they are doing and of how they look. The bad actor and the star are two tools that a director can employ to prize perception free of the tyranny of narrative. And if the bad actor's dissonance regarding his or her surroundings and role can serve to prepare an audience for the star's own type of incongruity, the star is not necessarily the end to which everything else is subordinate. Our patience, even fascination with a star is our patience and fascination with the sheer act of perception.

If Dietrich can be differentiated from the bad actor, it is without folding her into the company of good actors. James Naremore, in *Acting in the Cinema*, seeks to explicate what sets her apart:

Neither a realist nor a comic, she inhabits a realm where visible artifice becomes the sign of authenticity. She also challenges our ability to judge her acting skill, because her image is unusually dependent on a controlled, artful *mise-en-scène*.[15]

Naremore's contention that Dietrich's acting eludes judgment by the more familiar criteria of the profession is at its most tenable when it is her films with Sternberg that are taken as the test case: the backdrop of these works is such that it conspires with the oddities and extravagances of her performance. In her collaborations with other directors, Dietrich often appears as though she has wandered unwittingly from her proper domain. With her unflattering Raggedy Ann coiffure as the bar-top singer Frenchy in George Marshall's *Destry Rides Again* (1939)—a film that salvaged her standing at the box office after several years of commercial misfires—she in effect presents a critique and travesty of her Sternbergian persona of a chic nightclub entertainer: her world has disappeared, leaving her to minister to the diversionary needs of brawling cowboys. The astonishing verisimilitude of the choreography of the crowd scenes in *Destry Rides Again* has the paradoxical consequence less of anchoring Dietrich's Frenchy in a fully articulated environment than of setting her adrift. This, however, is not prejudicial to the narrative, because it invests the character with a vulnerability that helps explain her decisions in relation to the outsider Destry (James Stewart).

Sternberg, who was frequently punitive in his demands on Dietrich as a performer, shows by contrast a far greater care for her image. He does not explore the characterological implications of casting her in roles that can only jar with her stardom. This is not to suggest that she never deviates from "type" in the films they made together. When, for instance, she is reduced to destitution in *Blonde Venus* (1932), Sternberg's interest lies arguably less with Dietrich's characterization of Helen Faraday than with proliferating her modes of display. The result is not a callous aestheticization of vagrancy—Sternberg and Dietrich eschew their customary wryness in this sequence—even as a psychologically coherent portrait of Helen Faraday remains out of reach. In Sternberg's cinema, the concern with spectacle does not indicate a foreclosure of ethical and sociopolitical questions. How the aesthetic is to be understood in his films, if it can no longer be defined negatively by the suspension of these questions, is not to be answered without a reassessment of appearance in its relationship to truth and morality.

Sternberg's cinema, with its assiduous nurturing of spectacle for its own sake, amounts to an artistic translation of the moviegoer's experience of the disabling of the sensorimotor nexus. Perception here is not the precursor to action. But that is not the same as deferring action and obfuscating its possibility and necessity. Sternberg saw himself neither as propagandist nor as entertainer: the objective of his films consists no more in inculcating a practical stance on the world outside the cinema than in the denial of such a world in favor of the unreflective rush of consumerist pleasure. There is an ethical self-subsistence to what Sternberg understands and makes of spectacle. Recounting the aftermath of a screening of one of his films in Locarno in 1960, Sternberg claims that the Czech actor Jana Brejchová, "brought up under Soviet influence, and probably not hitherto exposed to something that abstains from all political ideology, was not unmoved by a cinematic philosophy which might pose many a problem but never offers any solution."[16] The remark is enlightening, if also easily misread. Sternberg does not boast of having lifted the veil of ideology just as he does not insinuate, in keeping with a Cold War trope, that ideology was endemic to the Eastern Bloc. Aiming to make sense of Brejchová's overwrought response to the screening, Sternberg is, of course, not so modest as to pretend that any Hollywood film would have had the same effect. If, within the production constraints and conditions of capitalist cinema, Sternberg believed he was able to refrain from political ideology, it was not because he trusted in his capacity to provide a clear-sighted depiction of what is—it is rather because he does not instrumentalize cinema. The discomfort with didacticism conveyed in Sternberg's recollection of his meeting with Brejchová is furthermore not that of the realist filmmaker who considers it politically dishonest, even reactionary, to propose fictional solutions to the social problems he or she portrays. (The salvation that the narrative might afford an invented character is scarcely transferable to the flesh-and-blood human beings whose lives are intertwined with these problems.) Sticking to the problem is not the preserve of the realist. Sternberg's problems are the problems of perception and appearance that the cinema is uniquely equipped to pose.

The cinematic philosophy that Sternberg stakes out applies itself to these problems. The qualifier "cinematic" denotes both the content and the medium of Sternberg's philosophical investigation. To gauge the justness of Sternberg's self-ascription is a matter less of looking for cinematic treatments of previously delineated philosophical positions than of inquiring how these films stay with their own problems, open them out, and delve into them. If there is something irresolvably cinematic to the philosophy of Sternberg's films, a textual analysis of his work, needless to say, will not be able to transcribe it seamlessly into the traditional verbal medium of philosophy. Any transcription at all, however, that fails to testify to the alterity of its starting point or inspiration is effectively redundant.

Sternberg is pre-eminently a studio director. His partiality to studio shoots is bound up with the greater degree of artistic oversight that a custom-built environment promises a filmmaker. By shooting on a studio soundstage, Sternberg avoids several difficulties, such as the inconstancy of natural light, the inquisitiveness of onlookers, and the unpredictability of ambient sound. He avoids these difficulties in order not to avoid any problem whatsoever, but rather to draw closer to the problems that interest him. The studio is a laboratory where Sternberg can conduct controlled experiments in cinematic spectacle. Shooting in a studio does not entail withdrawing from the world and cancelling the camera's relationship with the profilmic (Sternberg's films do not aspire to resemble cartoons). What the studio allows Sternberg to optimize is the spectacle of the profilmic that he uncovers in Dietrich. He makes a spectacle out of her resistance. This resistance of hers is emblematic of the resistance with which the profilmic is, by nature, simultaneously contrafilmic: that which appears before the camera as a body or event for it to record likewise stands apart from it, a proof of the camera's mimetic insufficiency. It is a resistance and agency whose trace and scene are to be found in the cinematic image itself. Dietrich's face is photogenic in a more exacting sense than usual, because it is a face in which the camera sees reflected the specific difference of its twofold condition of the technologically wondrous and the putatively subartistic. In its sovereignty, Dietrich's face confirms, even proclaims the camera's exposure to something outside of its power and capacity for invention, but this finitude and humbling of the camera, which demarcates it from the traditional arts (sculpture, literature, and so on can generate a mimetic relation or reference for their images from their own respective media), is also essential to the camera's claim as a technological device to be adequate—wondrously so—to the reproduction of reality. The presence of the face in the cinematic image is always also, in a manner of speaking, its absence.

According to Sternberg, a contrariness has entered into the historical choice to locate the major film studios in Hollywood: "The motion picture began by using one light, the light of the sun, and it followed the sun to California where it shone the brightest and where the clouds were rare—and where it is now used the least."[17] The director who opts for studio lighting balks at having to accommodate the sun's ungovernable expressiveness: the latter is not the competition that Sternberg wants. With the enhanced command of lighting that the artifice of the studio brings about, Sternberg is able to complicate the visual texture of the profilmic. Given that the anthropocentrism of the studio in enforcing the abdication of the sun corresponds to a multiplication of the sources of light, the tyranny of the studio director is at the service of a regional suspension of the monological principle of our solar system. In Sternberg's films, objects and faces start to glow as though of themselves in a democratization of the visible world. This confected bioluminescence of the profilmic underscores a given object's or person's standing within a scene. The lighting, however, is motivated by Sternberg's sense of spectacle and composition. Where Sternberg differs from many other studio directors is that his use of artificial lighting is not dictated by the goal of closing the gap between the profilmic and the narrative: a prop is not rendered conspicuous solely because a plot point depends on it.

Narrative is thus not allowed to ease itself into the place vacated by the banished sun in a formal perpetuation of its monarchy.

But does Sternberg flout the conventions of narrative in his films with Dietrich merely so that his female star might all the better stake her claim to centrality? The pluralism of the visual field will then turn out to be specious, given that a single organizational law can be adduced for the apparent anarchy. Compared with his collaborations with Dietrich, Sternberg's other films show themselves less eager to indulge in deviations from the accepted modes of cinematic storytelling. These works are not so-called star vehicles; they do not belong to the genre in which the narrative is driven into the ground with an eye to providing an unimpeded view of the lead. Even as he displays every care in doing justice as much to the nuances as to the paroxysms in the performance that Emil Jannings gives in *The Last Command* (1928) or Charles Laughton in the unfinished *I, Claudius* (1937), Sternberg does not let the whole revolve around their star turns to the detriment of the narrative. If Dietrich seems to have induced in Sternberg a different practice and approach to filmmaking, it is not the case that he merely substituted her star persona for narrative as a given film's organizing principle. The aura of independence with which she is endowed escapes being attributed to a star's insusceptibility to his or her role's fictional predicament. The narrative anarchy of mute objects that colludes with her assertion of autonomy also informs how this autonomy is to be understood. It is an independence not from spectacle, but rather within it. A close reading of Dietrich's last four films with Sternberg will bear this out.

These four films—*Shanghai Express* (1932), *Blonde Venus* (1932), *The Scarlet Empress* (1934), and *The Devil Is a Woman* (1935)—more perfectly realize certain themes and figures that are touched upon only more or less in passing in the three earlier collaborations. *Dishonored* (1931), the third of the series, travels the least distance in surveying the possibilities of Marlene as autonomous spectacle: the instability of her appearance is narratively recuperated or at least rendered more manageable, because her adoption of various disguises and her changes in self-presentation are explicable in terms of the missions she carries out as a spy for the Austrian government.[18]

Between *Dishonored* and *Shanghai Express*, while Dietrich was on vacation in Europe, Sternberg directed *An American Tragedy* (1931) for Paramount. He was brought in as a last-minute replacement for Sergei Eisenstein after the studio bosses had rejected the latter's treatment of Theodore Dreiser's 1925 novel of the same name. The film is revealing in what it shows of Sternberg as a director in the absence of Dietrich in what is nonetheless a variation of the femme fatale storylines with which the two had become associated, however unfairly, in the public imagination. Never quite embracing the part of being a male vamp, Clyde Griffiths (Phillips Holmes) is a pale imitation of Marlene and he is such by design. Not only is there an inversion of gender, but there is also a relocation of agency from appearance to effect with the result that, counterintuitive as it may initially seem, agency is attenuated. To watch *An American Tragedy* together with the Dietrich collaborations is to be confronted with a thesis concerning the domain in which autonomy is at its most plausible. The autonomy that Dietrich asserts by means of her appearance is at one with the autonomy of appearance itself. Semblance, in its suspension over the world of facts, does not straightforwardly buckle to causality. In Sternberg's films, Dietrich's responsibility for the fate of the men around her is at most indirect, given that the misfortunes that they hatch for themselves require a cause more substantial than an appearance. The downward trajectory of Immanuel Rath (Emil Jannings) in *The Blue Angel*, the film that comes closest to depicting Dietrich as a femme fatale, is plotted, for instance, by the series of decisions taken by the male protagonist—as Lola Lola clarifies in the number she is singing when Rath first enters the nightclub, a flame cannot be held to account for the moths that resolve to hurl themselves into it.

What Clyde Griffiths lacks by way of an appearance of autonomy, he can make up for only through deeds. Yet in the commission of the murder for which he is ultimately convicted, he still falls short of full agency. It is an act he had planned, but whose execution in the face of a change of heart or loss of nerve is precipitated on him by circumstances. Knowing that his fiancée, Roberta Alden (Sylvia Sidney), cannot swim, he rows her out on a lake in the Adirondacks with an eye to staging her accidental drowning. Once she is out of the way, he will be able to pursue his relationship with the wealthy Sondra Finchley (Frances Dee). The scene is reminiscent of F. W. Murnau's *Sunrise* (1927): in both films a man abandons his original intention to drown one woman for the sake of his interest in another, but the external world, as though slow on the uptake, sets itself to realizing the renounced desire. In *An American Tragedy*, the discovery of the abandoned plan prompts a distraught Roberta to lose her balance. And when the boat consequently capsizes, and Clyde sees her struggling in the water, he all too quickly convinces himself that the real decision has already been made and he chooses to swim off without rescuing her.

For Eisenstein, his replacement's adaptation foregoes any critique of American society.[19] Sternberg does not look through the characterless Clyde Griffiths to the economic forces that explain his rootlessness, social climbing, and casual amoralism. But he does not look as far as these forces because he prefers to dwell on Clyde's vacuity and to handle it as a properly cinematic phenomenon. This is a different demystification from that usually undertaken by the naturalist novel, where the hero's agency is uncovered as a collection of subterranean mechanisms that he can neither master nor understand—he only appears to act in his own story. Measured against Sternberg's Marlene, Clyde does not even appear.

An American Tragedy is proof of the sobriety and canniness of Sternberg's attitude toward spectacle: it is not the automatism of a style in which he is ensnared. Eisenstein was to dismiss Sternberg's adaptation as a commonplace detective drama, but the minimalism and austerity of the film have less to do with a hard-boiled adherence to the facts than with the withdrawal of appearance. *An American Tragedy* is a contribution to apophatic cinema, a work of mourning in which Clyde Griffiths holds open the empty space of the visible. He is the Marlene who is missing. Like Marlene, he turns heads wherever he goes, but unlike Marlene, who is the confidante, so to speak, of her own appearance, the impact of his looks routinely catches him off guard. Sternberg takes few pains to establish the credibility of Clyde's attraction for the women who cross his path: the elaborate machinery of glamor assembled for Dietrich in her earlier outings at Paramount is not brought to bear on Phillips Holmes. Admittedly, there is one moment in the film at which Clyde approaches the self-assured seductiveness of Sternberg's Marlene. Having kept Roberta at a distance in response to her refusal to invite him up to her room, Clyde reads the note that out of desperation she has passed him in the workshop and fixes upon her a stare full of sexual avowal. Yet given the note's acquiescence to Clyde's earlier demands, the solicitation in his stare is superfluous and as cowardly as it is brazen. In its knowingness, in its conjoined impudence and languor, this close-up of Clyde is out of keeping with his otherwise stolidly impassive character and comes across as a citation of Dietrich dropped into proceedings. The effect is of Clyde's having sent a surrogate to his meeting with his own appearance.

When after *An American Tragedy* Sternberg resumed his collaboration with Dietrich, he renewed and deepened his engagement with the question of appearance. The four masterpieces that they went on to make together differ markedly from one another in terms of setting, period, genre, design, and style of acting. What they share is a preoccupation with spectacle as a horizon of human interaction. Appearance has its own code of conduct, its own requirement for equity that a character must learn and attempt to observe if trust is to win its way free from fact and disbelief. This is the lesson that Sternberg has Dietrich impart and that he also imbibes from her. Remaining loyal to its message, yet in *Destry Rides Again* finding herself in a cinematic world unreceptive to it, she declares: "Never mind what I am."

It is well known that La Rochefoucauld repeated this maxim of the ancients: "Neither the sun nor death can be looked directly in the face." But perhaps the question is: What thing *can* be looked directly in the face? If looking something "in the face" means seeing its "truth" or "evidence," then there is never any direct face-to-face. Every face is a bedazzlement, terrible and marvelous.

JEAN-LUC NANCY

I have therefore found it necessary to deny *knowledge*, in order to make room for *faith*.

IMMANUEL KANT, *Critique of Pure Reason*, B xxx

1 *Shanghai Express*
MAKING ROOM FOR FAITH IN APPEARANCES

SHANGHAI EXPRESS WAS to be commercially the most successful of Dietrich and Sternberg's collaborations. Topping the box office for 1932, it amassed Sternberg the studio capital that he then proceeded to burn through with increasingly extravagant productions. Its storytelling is Sternberg at his most controlled. That this does not come at the price of a dimming of his signature on the film is because the screenplay by Jules Furthman, based on an unpublished story by Harry Hervey, ventures out to meet Sternberg on the home territory of his preoccupations and obsessions. Although *The Scarlet Empress* and *The Devil Is a Woman* were soon to overtake it in the direction of exorbitant spectacle, *Shanghai Express* has its cast engage with and comment on the problems and possibilities of appearance and make-believe. It is a contribution to a metacinema of the studio shoot.

In the war-ravaged China that Paramount threw together in southern California, a baroque density of design passes itself off as realism and a multinational assembly of characters, like that of Agatha Christie's later *Murder on the Orient Express* (1934), boards a train where almost no one is as he or she seems. For all their centrality to what in many other films would count as the action, the murder and its perpetrator, Hui Fei (Anna May Wong), are downplayed. (One could find fault with Sternberg and Furthman's ingenuity in contriving yet another excuse for marginalizing non-European actors in Hollywood.) In *Shanghai Express* the series of unmaskings and revelations are not stages on the way to truth: the destination is an embracing of appearances and the many close-ups, with their fastidiousness and fervor, do not even aspire to that looking in the face whose very possibility Jean-Luc Nancy disputes in any case.[1]

Toward the end of the film there is an exchange between Shanghai Lily (Dietrich) and the Reverend Carmichael (Lawrence Grant) wherein she sets out the peculiar terms on which she is prepared to revive her relationship with Captain Donald Harvey (Clive Brook). Having offered herself to Henry Chang (Warner Oland), the self-described commander-in-chief of the revolution, in exchange for Harvey's release, Shanghai Lily has demonstrated she is not the unfeeling sex worker that many of her fellow passengers, including the lover from whom she was estranged five years before, had taken her to be. Nevertheless, she upholds for herself—and, by extension, for the cinema of spectacle of which she is the focus—the claim of sheer appearance to be appreciated for its own sake:

CARMICHAEL SITTING DOWN: *You prayed last night, probably for the first time in years.*
　　Close shot of CARMICHAEL, very earnest.
CARMICHAEL: *This morning you were to shamelessly leave with Chang. There's something wrong there. You can't tell me that a human being can do two things like that within six hours!*
　　Close shot of LILY, impressed by CARMICHAEL's earnest approach.
LILY: *Although it's nobody's affair but mine, I might tell you if you promise not to repeat it.*
CARMICHAEL OFF: *Of course I won't repeat it.*
　　Very close shot of CARMICHAEL.
CARMICHAEL: *I came in here to find out for myself. I'm not interested in the others.*
　　Very close shot of LILY, serious and composed.
LILY: *He was going to deprive Captain Harvey of his eyesight. I had no other choice.*
　　CARMICHAEL gets to his feet and faces LILY.
CARMICHAEL: *Does Captain Harvey know that?*
LILY: *Does he act as if he did?*
CARMICHAEL: *He certainly does not. Despite the fact that I gave you my word not to tell anyone, I'm going to tell him this.*
LILY: *You're not going to do anything of the kind.*
　　Very close shot of LILY, smiling ironically.
LILY: *Mr Carmichael, it may seem odd for me to use your language, but it's purely a question of faith. You see, once upon a time, we loved each other.*
　　Very close shot of CARMICHAEL, listening closely.
　　Very close shot of LILY, her face partly obscured in a cloud of cigarette smoke.

LILY: *We parted, and I threw my life away because I didn't care to bargain for love with words. I haven't changed since then and neither has he.*

Close shot of CARMICHAEL looking down.

CARMICHAEL: *You're still in love with him, aren't you?*

Close shot of LILY, suddenly open.

LILY: *Yes.*

Very close shot of CARMICHAEL, earnest and sympathetic.

CARMICHAEL: *Is he still in love with you?*

Very close shot of LILY slightly bitter.

LILY: *I doubt it.*

CARMICHAEL slides the door of the compartment back as he prepares to leave.

CARMICHAEL: *You're right. Love without faith, like religion without faith, doesn't amount to very much.*[2]

Even though Shanghai Lily's interlocutor is a Protestant missionary (and an irascible one at that), he takes no umbrage at the parody and profanation of Christianity in her reference to faith. Faith is here being called upon to exercise itself not in the anticipation of knowledge, but rather in the refusal of knowledge already available. As far as Shanghai Lily is concerned, what appears is never to give way to what is. This is not the faith of Pauline expectation: "For now we see through a glass, darkly; but then face to face: now I know in part; but then shall I know even as also I am known."[3] Indeed, it has more in common with the trust to which Lorelei Lee (Marilyn Monroe) considers herself entitled in Howard Hawks's *Gentlemen Prefer Blondes* (1953): "Aren't you even gonna say you're sorry? I won't fall in love with a man who won't trust me, no matter what I do."

Sternberg and Dietrich's fourth outing is a moral tale on the proper treatment of appearances. Shanghai Lily declines to be loved on the basis of knowledge: if she is to be loved, it must be on faith. But faith in what? Having broken off his liaison with the woman who was to become Shanghai Lily and whom he still calls by her earlier name of Magdalen, Donald Harvey is not to be afforded a glimpse of the true self that will correct the misinterpretation of appearances that triggered the "smash-up" (as he terms it) of their relationship. He is not to learn that she is in fact better than he assumed her to be. One might be tempted to think that she is merely resentful that he had not earlier given her the benefit of the doubt and that out of pique she now spurns the opportunity to set him straight concerning her character. But she, too, wants to believe, to be able to trust in Captain Harvey's faith. Love, rather than resentment and pique, describes what is at stake for her, at least in her own eyes. Captain Harvey's "error" was not so much that he had misinterpreted appearances as that he had moved beyond them at all: knowledge of Shanghai Lily's true character, of the ethical subject encapsulated in an act of sexual self-sacrifice to a third party, cannot make good this initial mistake. What it means for Captain Harvey to have faith in her is for him to love her as she appears to be, in the phantasm of her spectacle in contradistinction to the false no less than to the true self that can be said to lie behind it. The world of appearances, if it is to receive its due, must become an object of faith: it cannot be known but it can be believed in.

Dietrich's Shanghai Lily and, a generation later, Monroe's Lorelei Lee demand to be trusted, despite any evidence that might serve to ground an argument for their untrustworthiness (Lorelei's fiancé retorts exasperatedly: "That's being unreasonable"). A trust that disregards all countervailing evidence is more a form of willful credulousness and must deem itself complicit in any ensuing misfortune: the willful blindness with which a mid-twentieth-century husband might go along with being cuckolded, for instance, attests to resignation rather than trust. For her part, Shanghai Lily is not asking for a license for promiscuity and fraudulently passing it off as faith. She demands to be trusted even in defiance of the evidence of her trustworthiness that her good deed on behalf of Captain Harvey constitutes. What is left to motivate trust if all evidence is ruled inadmissible? As the faith that Shanghai Lily seeks from Captain Harvey is to be placed specifically in her, it is not a matter of a change in his attitude toward other people in general. It is to be a faith with the partiality of love. That which is left to account for this partiality when she withdraws the truth of her behavior from consideration is her appearance.

Unlike Judy Barton (Kim Novak) in Hitchcock's *Vertigo* (1958), Shanghai Lily wants to be loved for who she appears to be rather than for who she is. Whereas Judy Barton struggles against the recreated illusion of Madeleine Elster that John "Scottie" Ferguson (James Stewart) longs to foist upon her, Shanghai Lily does not attempt to stand back from her image. In light of the conversation with Carmichael quoted above, the final scene of the film, in which Shanghai Lily is reconciled with her former lover, turns on Harvey's making peace with her appearance. He has not been apprised of what she engaged to perform in defense of his eyesight, and she has not committed herself to a reform of her conduct.[4] Because nothing has changed, if there is to be a reconciliation, it can come about only through his leap of faith. Paul's distinction here does not hold: "For we walk by faith, not by sight."[5] For Captain Harvey to have faith in Shanghai Lily, he also must be able to see her: the preservation of his sight is thus pivotal in more than one respect to her recovery of his affections. She must be seen to be believed, but for her to be believed and not known she has to be seen in a particular way, as an affair of light and shade to which no truth claims adhere.

Even with its concluding suggestion that an open marriage is in the offing, *Shanghai Express* is not easily reduced to a louche pre-Code take on bourgeois sexual morality. Sternberg's film is a meditation on the distinctiveness of the phenomenal realm as concentrated in the image of Dietrich. The comportment named "faith" in Furthman's screenplay addresses appearance in its difference from reality. Appearance as such cannot be known. It can be believed, but once it is known, it ceases to be appearance and turns into reality. It is this step that Shanghai Lily—and one might add: Sternberg—endeavors to ward off. This is a cinema that asks to be believed in while yet discounting any equivalence between belief and knowledge. The spectacle does not set out to impose itself on reality, to interpose itself between the viewer and what is, for such a conflation would annul the distinctness of the comportment it craves. The film wants to hover and to dance and, gathering together all its desires for suspending the downward pressure of the real and the knowledge of what is, it invests them in the appearance of Dietrich.

Having faith in an appearance is not the same as being duped by an appearance, because the latter involves a knowledge claim that happens to be wrong. The faith to which Shanghai Lily appeals likewise cannot be identified with an agnosticism with regard to any knowledge claims that might be made on behalf of appearances: the indifference of such an approach can scarcely be regarded compatible with the affect of love. Faith in an appearance as appearance is a pledge to relish it and to orient one's actions in relation to it. It is the cathexis that remains of belief in an appearance when belief is pried loose of a knowledge claim. It is more than the pleasure of spectatorship: the passivity of the latter, even if it grasps the appearance as appearance in contradistinction to the knowable, is apt to respect the boundaries between the aesthetic and practical attitudes. Shanghai Lily does not want from Captain Harvey merely recognition of her beauty (she receives this early on). The aesthetic attitude falls short of the faith that she is after inasmuch as it restricts itself to the observation of beauty: it keeps an appreciative distance from appearance instead of leaping into it.

In yearning to be believed rather than known, Shanghai Lily bids to situate herself resolutely within the realm of appearances. Like the wives of Eros, Bluebeard, Lohengrin, and Lot, Captain Harvey is expected to rein in any epistemic ambitions he might harbor. Shanghai Lily's wariness in the face of knowledge of her good deed is not a wariness that she will cease to be lovable on its account—on the contrary, it is closer to the uncomfortable conjecture that the more she is known for who she is, the less she will appear. Her beauty risks suffering an eclipse, because the pure appreciation of beauty, as Kant contends in §4 of the third *Critique* (1790), is at odds with an interest in the *existence* of a phenomenon: interest can ground a judgment of the good or of the agreeable, but not a pure aesthetic judgment of free beauty.[6] The genuine recipient of Shanghai Lily's remarks to the Protestant minister is, so to speak, Sternberg himself, for these remarks announce the character's surrender to his indefatigable and single-minded care over her appearance (as a character in the film, Shanghai Lily, in another but not unrelated respect, only comes into being with Sternberg's care over Dietrich's appearance). The wish to appear and nothing more to Captain Harvey, in other words, to someone who has had no input into her appearance and whose line of work does not revolve around the shaping and enhancing of appearances, is by comparison little short of unfathomable. Admittedly, Shanghai Lily's confidence in the power of her appearance, like Lorelei Lee's in *Gentlemen Prefer Blondes*, is not misplaced.

As a hymn to appearances and as an endorsement of the bond between the director and his star, *Shanghai Express* is not especially attached to the reality it depicts. Its salutes to the sore points of bourgeois convention, while they are unmissable, also lend themselves to being reckoned simply as cinematic devices. Impropriety supercharges visibility. Dietrich's character is introduced in the film as a "coaster," which being a novel expression requires its own elucidation: "a woman who lives by her wits along the China coast."[7] That this, in turn, signifies prostitution is left to the audience to infer from the other characters' indignant reactions to her as well as from whatever easily cracked code might be imagined to reside in

FIGURE 1.1. A rebus of prostitution composed from a spider's web, tail feathers of Mexican fighting cocks, the immune responses of oysters, and the skins of tropical frogs: Marlene Dietrich as Shanghai Lily in *Shanghai Express* (dir. Josef von Sternberg, Paramount Pictures, 1932).

the wardrobe of jet black feathers, silks, and two-toned leather gloves with which Travis Banton, chief costume designer at Paramount, fitted her out. The subject of prostitution is never broached, although Furthman's screenplay takes and gives delight in skirting it. One example of this mischievousness occurs early on when Mrs. Haggerty (Louise Closser Hale) thinks of joining Shanghai Lily and Hui Fei in their compartment. That what Shanghai Lily mishears Mrs. Haggerty saying is that she keeps a bawdy house is a joining of the dots by means of which an audience is made coauthor of the film's debauched subtext:

> MRS HAGGERTY: *I have a boarding house in Shanghai.*
> HUI FEI hardly reacting to MRS HAGGERTY's prattle.
> MRS HAGGERTY OFF: *Yorkshire pudding is my speciality* . . . .
> MRS HAGGERTY hands out cards to LILY and HUI FEI.
> MRS HAGGERTY continuing: *. . . and I only take the most respectable people.*
> LILY looks at the card which MRS HAGGERTY has handed to her.
> LILY: *Don't you find respectable people terribly dull?*
> MRS HAGGERTY is startled out of her wits.
> MRS HAGGERTY: *You're joking, aren't you? I've only known the most respectable people. You see, I keep a boarding house.*
> LILY looks innocently puzzled.
> LILY: *What kind of a house did you say?*
> MRS HAGGERTY looks very indignant.
> MRS HAGGERTY ICILY: *A boarding house!*
> A look of amused comprehension comes over LILY's face.
> LILY thus enlightened: *Oh!*[8]

When, in a much later scene, Mrs. Haggerty again refers to her boarding house, Sternberg cuts to Donald Harvey looking quizzical, thereby instituting between him and Shanghai Lily a parapractical solidarity. The film in general is more interested in the semblance and intimation of immorality than in its reality.

In making a show of immorality on which it does not follow through, *Shanghai Express* engages in one of the less commonly remarked species of hypocrisy. Many of Shanghai Lily's fellow travelers, by contrast, turn out to be hypocrites of the stock type. When they first encounter Shanghai Lily and Hui Fei, they puff themselves up over their own pretensions to moral superiority only, one after the other, to be caught out in a lie, a deception, or a swindle. Their outrage at traveling with alleged prostitutes does not so much channel as pay lip service to the Catholic coalition soon to begin agitating in earnest for a strict enforcement of the Production Code. Given the prospect of walkouts and demands for ticket refunds, having one or more characters within the frame preempt an audience's condemnation of prostitution was a way for a film to win a little time to approach the topic.

With regard to Hui Fei, sitting smoking on her own in a long-sleeved cheongsam, a viewer who is not conversant with the China of the period and thus unable to make sense of its signifying systems might be tempted to take on trust a Christian missionary's judgment of her appearance:

CARMICHAEL: *I won't share a compartment with this woman.*
PORTER: *Change you tonight, sir.*
CARMICHAEL ANGRILY: *You'll change me now! I haven't lived for ten years in this country not to know a woman like that when I see one! Get me another compartment. Take my luggage out of here!*

As he exits the compartment, Hui Fei flicks the ash from her cigarette, implying an equivalence between it and a Doctor of Divinity's pretensions to moral panic. Sternberg gives her the final "word" in this encounter: her close-up rebuffs his authority to pass judgment on her appearance. When Shanghai Lily thereafter joins her, silently pulling down the blinds to the corridor, it is as though introductions are unnecessary for two women whose social standing is similar and unmistakable.

In *Shanghai Express* Sternberg instrumentalizes the physical flurry of indignation among the passengers to highlight the comparatively stationary figure of Dietrich (Wong maintains even greater reserve in these early scenes). Once the expression of their animus has fulfilled this function, her accusers are free to dispense with their moral credibility. Their own claims to respectability do not bear up under examination. Shanghai Lily's fellow passengers also deal in appearances. The German Eric Baum (Gustav von Seyffertitz), having presented himself as the proprietor of a coal mine, is exposed as an opium dealer. The Midwestern racist and compulsive gambler Sam Salt (Eugene Pallette) passes himself off as wealthy by means of what are, in fact, imitation jewels. The French Major Lenard (Émile Chautard), whom Sam Salt dubs a sardine inspector, has no right to the uniform he wears, having been dishonorably discharged. Even the forbidding Mrs. Haggerty does not balk at ignoring rules where her dog Waffles is concerned.

The inversion of the established social values of appearances is at its starkest in the following character assessment, which Henry Chang offers Shanghai Lily:

LILY: *You made me an offer to leave with you. Does it still hold good?*
Close shot of CHANG's crafty face.
CHANG: *I wouldn't trust you . . .*
Close shot of LILY, with the soldier guarding her.

CHANG CONTINUING OFF: . . . *from here to the door. What assurance have I . . .*
 Close shot of CHANG.
CHANG CONTINUING: . . . *you won't trick me?*
 Close shot of LILY, still guarded by the soldier.
LILY: *I give you my word of honour.*
CHANG: *A man is a fool to trust any woman, but I believe a word of honour would mean*
 something to you.[10]

Chang's credulity is not dictated by the plot: having soldiers at his command, he does not have to rely on Shanghai Lily's word that she will leave with him in exchange for Captain Harvey's release. Chang opts to trust Shanghai Lily notwithstanding her reported history of "wrecking" a dozen men up and down the coast and his misogynistic prejudices regarding the faithfulness of women. He trusts her, not because he does not know any better, but rather perhaps because he wants more of her in return for Captain Harvey—not only the hard fact of the body that will henceforth remain in his possession, but also the appearance that discloses itself solely to those who trust. This would provide him with a motive for trusting her in particular, which he eschews in relation to the other passengers. Given that he has earlier declared to Sam Salt that he is not proud of his father's white blood, his decision to trust Shanghai Lily cannot be ascribed to any esteem for the higher standards of conduct that white society liked to imagine it observed and with which it flattered itself as pursuing a civilizing mission in the midst of its imperialist adventures.[11] The viewer is thus not encouraged to interpret his trust as recognition that Shanghai Lily has not gone as far "native" as many of her fellow passengers believe for her recovery into the folds of "good society" to be impossible (if the passengers on board the train are anything to go by, it cannot be taken for granted that such a society even exists).

Comparing *Shanghai Express* and John Ford's *Stagecoach* (1939), Gina Marchetti writes of narratives in which "the 'fallen woman,' herself equated with the savage land through which the vehicle of civilization passes, is saved and rejoins the civilization that shunned her."[12] Marchetti notes some of the ambiguities whereby *Shanghai Express* complicates the female character's supposed redemption by and for the love of a white male. But it is debatable whether *Shanghai Express* can pass for even an outlier of the genre Marchetti delineates. Shanghai Lily must first have belonged to the civilization that shunned her for her to be able to rejoin it. It is not clear where she is "at home." This is a constant in the films, because Sternberg tends to favor a mobile sense of Dietrich's exoticism. That which does not fit in attracts attention to itself: it is preconditioned to appeal to desires and curiosities for which the prevailing social environment denies an outlet.

Shanghai Express is an exercise in making Dietrich stand out. The exoticism of the setting does not annex her own exoticism. By stacking exoticisms, Sternberg mobilizes the powers of the eye. To the extent that a Chinese setting is unfamiliar it increases the effort that must be expended in order to perceive it. To the extent that it includes cultural inaccuracies in its design it also puts the eye of the knowing viewer on alert. Sternberg sacrifices realism to an athleticism of the eye, because a world that does not quite work—that is either too removed from a viewer's experience or is incoherent within itself—is more conducive to the apprehension of a phenomenon in its singularity.

Although Dietrich's character bears the name of a Chinese city, Sternberg does not resort to yellowface to try to fuse Shanghai Lily's exoticism with the larger exoticism of China. When Ruby Keeler appears in the "Shanghai Lil" sequence that Busby Berkeley directed for Warner Bros' *Footlight Parade* (1933), her use of yellowface is a less than creditable point of difference from the earlier film on whose coattails the number clearly wants to ride.[13] Berkeley and Sternberg are both artists for whom it is sufficient to nod toward the appearance of prostitution. If Ruby Keeler is unconvincingly Chinese, she is also implausible as a worldly prostitute. She soon abandons any reference to Dietrich's earlier performance to tap-dance on top of a bar with James Cagney. Through the injection of improbabilities into their films, Sternberg and Berkeley loosen the hold that reality has on the viewer's judgment. With her eyes wide open and flitting back and forth, Dietrich's characterization of Shanghai Lily at times borders on comedy without ever succumbing to evaluation by its criteria. Lacking any of Dietrich's archness or exoticism, Ruby Keeler is so much the "girl next door" that her revelation as Shanghai Lil in effect sends up the sexualization of foreign women (the sequence ends, furthermore, on a decidedly jingoistic note with drill formations that are shot from overhead and in which marchers hold up cards to compose images of the American flag and President Roosevelt).[14] If Sternberg also manages to avoid cloying the viewer with his adoration of Dietrich's image, it is because Dietrich herself resists this adoration—or, to put it differently, because Sternberg's favored image of Dietrich, the one he enlists her to create, conveys her aloofness toward the very business of image-making. There is a steady conversion or mutual reinforcement between the reserve of the performer regarding the technological manipulation of her image and the coolness of her roles in relation to bourgeois respectability.

Sternberg's cinema has a reason for being attracted to the figure of the prostitute, one that is inoperative in a novel. Depending on how seriously one takes Sternberg's claims for the sexual probity of his films, it might be considered the principal or even sole reason. Where Dietrich's characters merge with the prostitute is in calling attention to themselves. The assumptions and customs surrounding prostitution are put to use to render Dietrich more visible. As an art in whose advantage it is to develop a knack for catering to the weaknesses, habits, and enthusiasms of the human eye, cinema harbors an idiosyncratic but not unintelligible inquisitiveness with respect to the figure of the prostitute. The prostitute, however, who is discreet and inconspicuous, who does not solicit, makes for an unpromising ally for Sternberg's cinematic ambitions. The meretriciousness of a streetwalker is what is called for. Stereotypes are to be marshaled, as much for the ease with which they can be construed as for their specific content. Because this overtness is still not enough for Sternberg to saturate the frame with visibility, he combines it with Hollywood glamor and Dietrich's beauty. Were one to object that in the process he romanticizes prostitution, grossly misrepresenting the reality as it is experienced by the vast majority of female sex workers, Sternberg is in a position to deny (with the coyness that was to become second nature in the major studios) that he is concerned with anything more than prostitution as appearance. Sternberg and Dietrich toy with the appearance of prostitution for their own ends. They tap into its heightened visibility for the sake of a cinema of spectacle. Any flippancy that remains in this is inextricable from an audience's own substitution of this appearance for the reality.

This collusion with the self-magnifying visibility of the profilmic is not inconsistent with a passage in Sternberg's memoirs that has nonetheless been misread (by Mulvey among others) as a statement of cinematic formalism:

> Were I to instruct others how to use the camera, the first step would be either to project a film upside down or to show it so often that the actors and story become no longer noticeable, so that the values produced by the camera alone could not escape study. The camera collects all faults and virtues but is not responsible for them all.[15]

To acquire an insight into what the camera can achieve, according to Sternberg, it must be studied as far as possible in a kind of independence from the profilmic: inversion and repetition are means to this end if they manage to convert significance-laden objects within the world into blocks of light and shade to be handled as compositional elements. But what the camera on its own can bring to the experience of cinema does not encompass everything that can enliven the frame. What counts for Sternberg is less the exhibition of his own skill than the force of the image. He feels little temptation to restrict himself to a self-referential formalism of the camera. The camera's own contribution to visibility is to be built upon by choosing from the profilmic that which already possesses a talent, however raw and uncultivated, for attracting attention.

Sternberg's zeal for the demimonde in his films with Dietrich is a zeal for the cinematic absolute, for the maximally visible.[16] The image that never ceases to invite and to reward contemplation enjoys an absolute visibility that must be differentiated from straightforward perspicuousness and intelligibility, for that which we take in at a glance can quickly sink into a kind of invisibility. To make a star out of Dietrich, to have her move from the demimonde to the beau monde of transatlantic high society, is to add the visibility of celebrity to the visibility that was already hers. To treat this transition as finished business and to cast her henceforth in roles with nothing of the streetwalker and the flirt in them would, however, require Sternberg to relinquish some of his devices for vivifying the image. The work behind the visibility of the famous, given that it is largely performed out of sight (by money, connections, past deeds, and the like), leaves free within the frame the possibility for a different class of work on a different class of visibility. Needless to say, to propose that there is something more than aggression toward Dietrich in Sternberg's typecasting of her is not to discount this aggression, of which *The Devil Is a Woman* is on many grounds the culmination and breaking point.

In *Shanghai Express* Dietrich moves about in a luminiferous cloud of connotations and rumors mantling her with the appearance of a courtesan or vamp. Even the nonprofessional name of "Magdalen" by which Captain Harvey remembers her merely adds to this unstable network of associations (given that Dietrich herself was baptized "Marie Magdalene," the choice of name also plays on any presumed continuities between performer and role). Dietrich's character does not attempt to alter her appearance but rather denies that it was fair of her former lover to judge her on appearances—more precisely, to judge her by what he took to be the reality inferable from those appearances:

LILY PUZZLED: *Well, how have I changed?*

HARVEY: *I don't know. I wish I could describe it.*

LILY: *Well, Doc, I've changed my name.*

HARVEY: *Married?*

LILY: *No.*

    LILY shakes her head. Train bell.

LILY: *It took more than one man to change my name to Shanghai Lily.*

    HARVEY stares at her, his back to the window. Train bell.

HARVEY: *So you're Shanghai Lily!*

    LILY smiles. Train bell.

LILY: *The notorious white flower of China. You've heard of me and you always believed what you heard.*

Close shot of HARVEY, smiling ironically. Train bell.
HARVEY: *And I still do. You see, I haven't changed at all.*[17]

She later reproaches him for his gullibility and herself for the stratagem that brought it into play:

> LILY: *You left me without a word, purely because I indulged in a woman's trick to make you . . .*
> HARVEY is trying desperately hard to put a calm mask on his emotional disturbance.
> LILY continuing off: *. . . jealous.*
> LILY decides to admit to what seems to be the truth.
> LILY: *I wanted to be certain that you loved me; instead, I lost you. I suffered quite a bit, and I probably deserved it.*[18]

When five years earlier she put Captain Harvey's trust to the test, she learned that she could not be certain of his love. His lack of faith in her was matched by her own in him. As the desire for certainty had proved fatal for their relationship, she renounces it for herself and calls upon him to do so as well.

The reconciliation toward which Shanghai Lily strives is to take place within the horizon of appearances. Make-believe is the two-handed undertaking to which she invites Captain Harvey in the film's concluding lines in Shanghai's crowded railway station:

> HARVEY: *There's only one thing I want you to tell me, Magdalen.*
> LILY: *What's that?*
> HARVEY: *How in the name of Confucius can I kiss you with all these people around?*
> We see crowds of people passing to and fro through the station. HARVEY looks down at LILY, then uneasily at the people passing by.
> LILY: *But Donald, there's no one here but you and I. Besides, many lovers come to railroad stations to kiss without attracting attention.*[19]

Hesitant that she can persuade him to pretend that they are alone and can kiss without embarrassment, Shanghai Lily refers to the railway station on the other side of the Pacific that they are already pretending is not a Paramount sound stage. As a character in a work of fiction, Donald Harvey cannot help being caught up in a suspension of the authority of the senses' evidence. Shanghai Lily entreats him to come to terms with his own nature and circumstances, because to insist too vehemently on grabbing hold of the truth would be to risk tumbling out the other side of the set and its circumscribed zone of make-believe. The bourgeois marriage to which the pair seems hereafter headed need only appear to conform to the template of respectability. The film's ending accedes to convention and hollows it out.

In terms of a sympathetic understanding of Captain Harvey's reconciliation with the appearance of Shanghai Lily, however, the audience of *Shanghai Express* knows too much for its own good. It knows the motive for Shanghai Lily's arrangement with Chang and thus knows that she still loves Captain Harvey. But for the audience on the basis of this knowledge to approve Captain Harvey's decision to be reconciled with Shanghai Lily is for the audience not to understand his decision in its own motivations. By justifying the leap of faith, the audience's knowledge obstructs it from leaping with him, and the world of faith into which Shanghai Lily retires alone with Captain Harvey closes fast around the two of them.

The conclusion of *Shanghai Express* in effect asserts the privileges of make-believe against the hegemony of knowledge. If the audience falters in its judgment, concurring with Captain Harvey's decision to be reconciled but doing so for the wrong reasons, it is not because it knows too little—a condition that leaves the authority of knowledge as such uncompromised—but rather because it knows at all. The cognitive upper hand that the audiences of Greek drama hold over the hero in his tragic blindness still exists in Sternberg's film, although here love and not catastrophe is the price of ignorance. The happy ending points to a future of which the audience can know nothing. For the sake of the openness of this future, Shanghai Lily wants Captain Harvey to approach her in an attitude of faith. She does not ask to be forgiven. To seek forgiveness for past actions would be to concede the reality of those actions, even if only at the moment of their exculpatory erasure: forgiveness, as it places a check on the real to keep it from determining future interactions, is still too earthbound for her—forgiveness is faith with one foot on the ground, up to the ankle in mud. Forgiveness politely begs to differ from the verdict of knowledge whereas Shanghai Lily disputes that love even falls under knowledge's jurisdiction. "Love without faith, like religion without faith, doesn't amount to very much" is the thesis on which Shanghai Lily can agree with a missionary.

Yet the claim that knowledge, when available no less than when it is not, is to play no role in decision-making is a proposition more in keeping with the counsels whereby a succubus might hope to fend off exposure. A demonological reading of Shanghai Lily—and misogyny often has tipped over into demonology—will necessarily be insensitive, however, to the film's disregard of a reality separate from cinema. *Shanghai Express* neither subjects her preference of faith over knowledge to criticism nor calls it into question. She who wants to be believed grasps that in certain respects—as an image on a screen, a character in a fiction—she cannot be known. Here the audience in the cinema has an advantage over her fellow characters, for the knowledge it acquires of her motives in her dealings with Henry Chang is a knowledge that cannot puncture the make-believe of her appearance: learning who she really is in a fictional world does not shatter the illusion of the fiction itself. The audience's knowledge is a suspended knowledge, a kind of faith in the make-believe of the film. In this sense, the audience's knowledge of Shanghai Lily's motives does not preclude a sympathetic understanding of Captain Harvey's leap of faith.

But an audience can be told or shown something and still not believe it—in other words, it can know something about a character and nonetheless withhold belief from the work in which that character figures and in which the item of information is treated as true. It withholds belief because the given item of information is improbable according to historical or physical laws, because it is at odds with the conventions of the work's presumed genre, or because it is simply too dull to take seriously. For the audience of a work of fiction, knowledge and disbelief are not mutually exclusive. Its knowledge claims can be upheld by the work, but inasmuch as the audience does not buy into the story and characters the work depicts, disbelief accompanies the audience's knowledge. Exercising its faculties for belief, an audience decides whether to go along with the fiction presented to it. The permission that the work of art grants the audience (a permission grounded in the work's relative innocuousness) is to consult its pleasure in coming to a decision on whether or not to believe.

Like any fictional character, Shanghai Lily appeals to an audience to believe in her and rests that appeal on the pleasure she occasions. Although it goes without saying that the pleasure by which an audience member is won over for engaging with a fictional character need not have a visual interest, in the case of *Shanghai Express* Sternberg's conception of the nature of his protagonist's appeal clearly turns on her beauty. Sternberg courts the audience's attention for Shanghai Lily and for the film of which she is a part by meticulously showcasing her charms.

Ringing the changes of Dietrich's appearance, Sternberg is nonetheless not left open to the charge of an artistically ruinous fixation on his star: Furthman's screenplay, by its thematization of appearances, effectively excuses what would otherwise have all the earmarks of directorial self-indulgence. Each new scene becomes an opportunity for displaying Dietrich in a different combination of light and shade and in a different wardrobe. What action there is in the film struggles for visibility at the borders of its spectacle. The climactic plot point of *Shanghai Express*—Hui Fei's killing of Chang—is dealt with briskly in a shot lasting no more than twenty seconds. Filmed from behind as a darkened silhouette, Hui Fei stabs Chang twice in the back among the scenically unwarranted gauze curtains by means of which Sternberg was wont to layer space. As a consequence of Hui Fei's act, the train is free to resume its journey to Shanghai with both Captain Harvey and Shanghai Lily on board. When Shanghai Lily discovers that her offer to Chang has not earned her a hearing from Captain Harvey, she queries whether she is any better off for Chang's having been killed. Hui Fei tersely reminds her not to confuse her dominance of the spectacle of the film with centrality to its action:

> LILY: *I don't know if I ought to be grateful to you or not.*
> HUI FEI goes on playing solitaire.
> HUI FEI: *It's of no consequence. I didn't do it for you. Death cancelled his debt to me.*[20]

If the commercial choice of phrase bolsters her fellow passengers' conjecture that she is a prostitute, the fee she charges does not. Despite being aware of the price that the Chinese government has put on Chang's head, Hui Fei claims to have killed him in order to settle a personal debt. When the train finally arrives in Shanghai and the assembled Anglophone journalists are ready to launch her into the public realm, she brushes them off in Chinese. As though borne down by the weight of her action, she retreats from visibility. Not having acted, by contrast, Shanghai Lily is able to simply appear and thus to press her candidacy for faith in appearances.

This favoring of appearances over action in *Shanghai Express* entails a reassessment of the prevailing relationship in Hollywood films between character and continuity. A film that is shot in different settings can rely on its audience not to be disoriented by shifts in setting so long as there persist on screen one or more characters with whom the audience is already familiar. The character, as a physically mobile body within these different settings, is also a fixed point in relation to which the various locations of a film can be pieced together. For reorientation to take place by means of a character's appearance, the differences in a character's appearance among various scenes must not exceed the threshold beyond which identity becomes unrecognizable. A perceptual anthropocentrism enters into filmmaking with this characterological structuring device, although most Hollywood directors supplement it and contain it, relying on a deed and its consequences to provide another kind of continuity and to justify furthermore the changes in setting. For Sternberg, however, the deed and its afterlife are, as it were, the filmmaker's bad faith in relation to the structuring device that is a character's appearance. Not trusting in the appeal of their characters' appearances, other directors resort to narrative to try to maintain their audiences' interest until the final credits. Sternberg does not set the character's appearance against the disorientation brought about by a change in scene. He is less concerned with how it can stabilize perception of a new scene than with how the new scene can reinvigorate perception of the character's appearance. Backgrounds cease, strictly speaking, to be backgrounds once changes in location are determined by how a different décor might vivify the dynamics of a shot. Only a heavy-handed analysis of the permutations in Sternberg's close-ups of Dietrich could resolve them into a constant (the face) and variables (the backdrops). The face does not exist apart from its dialogues with its settings. Never the same object of perception from one moment to the next, the face extracts the communication of affects from a fluid and unpredictable collusion with masses of shadow and planes of light. It appears and gives itself up to the difference between appearance and truth through these transactions with disparate concrete spaces. Shot from above with her head thrown back as Captain Harvey leans down to kiss her on the open-air platform at the end of the train, Shanghai Lily is almost unrecognizable: Dietrich's face is less a point of continuity in the film than a site of experimentation.[21]

In examining various approaches to the close-up, Gilles Deleuze speaks of "Sternberg's anti-Expressionism" and "light's adventure with white":

> It is transparent, translucent or white space that has just been defined. Such a space retains the power to reflect light, but it also gains another power which is that of refracting, by diverting the rays which cross it. The face which remains in this space thus reflects a part of the light, but refracts another part of it. From being reflexive, it becomes intensive. Here there is something unique in the history of the close-up. The classical close-up ensures a partial reflection in so far as the face looks in a direction different from that of the camera, and thus forces the spectator to rebound on the surface of the screen. [. . .] But Sternberg seems to have been alone in doubling the partial reflection of a refraction, thanks to the translucent or white milieu that he was able to construct. [. . .] The close-ups of *Shanghai Express* form an extraordinary series of variations at the edges.[22]

It would be unreasonable to expect stills abstracted from the film to bear out Deleuze's claims in this passage. Just as it is not from any face that Sternberg manages to draw these same effects, Furthman's screenplay is likewise not incidental to the way the images of the film are construed. Deleuze's recourse to the terminology of optics cues its understanding of reflection and refraction to the fairness of Dietrich's skin and the emotional complexity of her face. And what the viewer, following Furthman, is to ask of the close-up is not the familiar question of what its object *is*: we move nearer all the better to believe in the appearance of what we are seeing.

Shanghai Lily wants her former lover to find room for faith. To make room for faith means, in this instance, to adopt a different lens through which to view phenomena. Captain Harvey is to see her as the viewer sees her, in close-up. The informational yields of the microscope and the telescope are separable from the affective intimacy of the close-up and its technological recreation of attention. As an object of faith, Shanghai Lily becomes visible in her irreducibility to the positive and the actual. She is that which appears while nevertheless being unknowable. If faith is not reserved for the unseen, it is because appearances themselves shelter in plain view something that is radically, rather than merely contingently unknowable. This unyielding unknowability of a phenomenon presenting itself to the senses and occupying a determinate position in time and space is what Alfred Baeumler designated in his 1923 monograph the problem of irrationalism in eighteenth-century aesthetics.[23] The beautiful is that which can be seen and yet not known. Its irrationality is a matter of the unavailability of a concept under which a given instance of the beautiful could be subsumed. The diversity of what we recognize as beautiful does not resolve into any common set of objective marks that likewise serves to differentiate the beautiful from the ugly or the aesthetically indifferent (whatever properties a specific aria, orchid, night sky, etc. might share—presuming that one judges these things to be beautiful—do not suffice to ring-fence them as a logical class, for what they share objectively they share also with arias that leave one cold, with flowers whose appeal is a riddle, with skies that do not quite "work," and so on). In the absence of a general concept of beauty we cannot tell ourselves that we recognize an instance of the beautiful by checking it for possession of certain objective marks known in advance; instead, we recognize it, as Dominique Bouhours and Gottfried Wilhelm Leibniz early on contended, by means of its *je ne sais quoi*.

Shanghai Lily is not asking Captain Harvey to leap blindly into the dark; he can trust his senses and learn faith from what he can see but not know. To live in beauty is to live in the suspension of knowledge; it is to live in a world of make-believe that is not necessarily a denial of reality. Dogma here does not populate faith's difference from knowledge (dogma is even faith's moment of weakness and self-doubt when it grapples for the firm ground that might replicate the certainty of knowledge). What faith enables by its circumscribing and containing of the domain of the knowable is the *chance* of a normative order. Every love affair contains a larval civilization in which we see and treat one another as more than the simple bodies moving in space that we know we are. In the *mise en abyme* of *Shanghai Express* the make-believe of cinematic fiction mirrors love's suspension of knowledge, substitutes itself for it, and recreates it within itself, offering it up to the public even as it spirits it away into the depths of the image.

"The gaze of the spectator in the darkened cinema auditorium has brought forth this being enveloped in gold, this wondrously mellow deep voice, and yet that which was brought forth was not the property of every single spectator, this woman was not created by the gaze as she-whom-everyone-wants, one for many, but rather she emerges, is put on display, her wings stir, and, actually, she looks back! She looks at you directly, she lays claim for herself—while being looked at—the prerogative of the gaze."

ELFRIEDE JELINEK

---

2 *Blonde Venus*
A SALE OF TWO BODIES

BASED ON A script by Jules Furthman and S. K. Lauren and released just seven months after *Shanghai Express, Blonde Venus* likewise touches on the selling of bodies and continues Dietrich and Sternberg's arraignment of bourgeois sexual morality. Although Ned Faraday (Herbert Marshall) denounces his wife, Helen (Dietrich), for the economic character of her dealings with the corrupt politician Nick Townsend (Cary Grant) and then has her hounded by the authorities from New York to Texas in pressing his claim to sole custody of their son Johnny (Dickie Moore), it is nonetheless Ned who first puts himself up for sale when he approaches an anatomical specialist in the film's third scene:

NED. Dr Pierce, I have a rather peculiar request to make. I want to sell you my body.

DR PIERCE. Why do you particularly want to sell it to me?

NED. Well, sir, in view of your reputation on this side of the water. I had an idea that my body in its present condition might be very interesting to you. Before as well as after death.

DR PIERCE. What's the matter with you?

NED. I've been poisoned by radium emanations.

Foreseeing his incapacitation through illness and death, Ned wants to sell his body in order to provide for his wife and son. He views his body as a good that is his alone to dispose of as he sees fit. He does not grant, however, that his wife has the same exclusive authority over her own body. That he is the beneficiary of her transactions with Nick Townsend does not at all mitigate what he perceives to be a violation of both his conjugal rights and his definition of motherhood.

Helen's motive for initiating a liaison with Nick Townsend is analogous to his in his proposition to Dr Pierce. She does not keep the money she raises for herself, giving it instead to her husband to cover the medical expenses that he otherwise has no hope of defraying. Literally speaking, she does not sell her body—at most she could be said to hire it out. By offering to make his body available to Dr Pierce while still alive, Ned cannot pretend that his commercial arrangement concerns an inanimate object. As he means to sell rather than merely hire his body out, it is hypocritical for him to condemn either prostitution for commodifying the human person or his wife for flouting his marital prerogative. The indignation and sense of grievance with which he drives Helen out of their home on his return from his successful treatment in Germany are not shot sympathetically. His face sinks ever deeper into shadow beneath the brim of his hat even as hers, with its faint suggestion of an insolent smile at his tirade, remains refulgent through the use of high-key lighting.[1] Ned and Helen's marriage, if it is to survive, will have to discover a way of thinking about sex and love that is not beholden to bourgeois morality's conjoint obsession with and horror of the body's salability.

The film's "happy ending," with Helen and Ned reconciled leaning over Johnny's cot, is, however, notoriously perfunctory. The discord between husband and wife has not so much been resolved as suppressed in favor of the fairy-tale romance that Helen and Ned have concocted as a bedtime story for their son. Exasperated with their unwillingness to play along, Johnny insists that they resume their established roles in the telling of how they first met. If they want him to fall asleep, they will need to convince him that they have made peace with each other. Yet as soon as he is asleep, they are at liberty to abandon the charade—if that is what it is. The film concludes before settling this issue.[2] Johnny's face is the last to be shown, as he starts to nod off contentedly. As portrayed by the six-year-old Dickie Moore, Johnny is arguably too old to sleep in a cot, but if he is to be infantilized, he can at least ensure that his parents are as well.

The fairy-tale romance with which the film begins and ends evokes a parallel fiction that Ned and Helen never manage to inhabit. Its rendering of events is vulnerable to criticism, for the words in which the bedtime story is related to Johnny do not correspond to the film version of the presumptive reality of Ned and Helen's first encounter. In the opening scene Ned and fellow American students are out hiking in the Black Forest. A magisterial tracking shot accompanies them: intervening tree trunks move across the frame from right to left like rolling vertical bands, underscoring the forward thrust of their motion. As Ned subsequently tells it, they come upon a dragon sitting in an automobile. The mimetic counterpart to this from the film's opening is the taxi driver at the wheel of his car whom a group of six actresses has engaged to wait for them while they swim nearby. What there is in him that might encourage the association with a dragon is little beyond his obdurate refusal to desert the women in order to give the exhausted hikers a lift into town (as a taxi's presence in the middle of the Black Forest strikes the students as the unbelievable fulfillment of a wish, it is itself an invitation to fantasy). In Ned's diegetic version the six actresses are six princesses. By transposing the incident to the register of the fairy tale, Ned whitewashes his unchivalrous extortion from Helen of a promise to meet him later that night. The women are naked and as they have to be back at the theater by six o'clock if they are not to lose their positions, she very grudgingly grants him his wish in return for being able to dress unmolested (the "real" story is thus less about rescue from a dragon than about falling into the clutches of one). Helen, in her contributions to Johnny's bedtime routine, does not contest Ned's version of events, but her palpable ire in the mimetic telling of their encounter amounts to a caveat against the fairy-tale romance's capacity to do justice to the ambivalences of their relationship.

The lesson that Ned must learn if his marriage is to recover does not involve putting aside the fairy-tale romance and confronting the prosaic, workaday reality of his wife as a fellow human being. Sternberg is too complicit in the production of the illusion of Dietrich for him to make out that the sobriety of disenchantment has anything to recommend it. Like *Shanghai Express, Blonde Venus* charts in part the consequences of a man's misjudgment of the woman he claims to love. Ned's error in both the bedtime story and the conventional sexual morality against whose criteria he judges Helen is his possessiveness. Because she does not belong to his world, she inevitably proves slippery to hold. Ned is closer to the mark when he calls her in their first exchange a water nymph, for she has more in common with a naiad or *rusalka* than with a fairy-tale princess or American housewife. The other world from which Ned tears Helen by marrying her and to which she returns in defiance of her husband is the stage.

The title of the film is the name that the nightclub proprietor Mr. O'Connor gives to Helen to help promote her act. Whereas in *Shanghai Express* it took more than one man to give Dietrich's character the name of Shanghai Lily, in *Blonde Venus* men never stop coming up with new labels for the woman whose original name is left undisclosed. Helen's seedy booking agent, Ben Smith (Gene Morgan), changes her surname from "Faraday" to "Jones." His reasoning is out of step with the name he actually proposes:

SMITH. What did you say your name was?

HELEN. Helen Faraday.

SMITH. No, we gotta get something different. Something unusual. Something that's easy to say and hard to forget. Jones. I got it. Helen Jones.

HELEN. But my name isn't Jones.

SMITH. What of it? My name ain't Smith either, but I get by just the same, don't I?

Helen will retain the stage name of Helen Jones even after she has severed all ties with her agent and is performing in Paris. Given that "Jones" in this period was anything other than unusual among surnames in the United States, Smith's choice is comically deflationary of the mystique of the theater (by contrast, thanks to the name's most famous bearer, "Faraday" would invest a nightclub act with not unbecoming connotations of electromagnetism). Yet *Blonde Venus*, as a whole, is not an indictment of the tinsel of show business. A feature of the films that Sternberg and Dietrich made together is that they want to have their cake and to eat it, too. Both director and star want to explore all the possibilities of the dramatic spectacle they are creating while also having the freedom to stand back from it, wryly insusceptible to its artifice and manipulation. Of course, the choice of "Jones" could equally be a declaration of confidence in the power of Dietrich to withstand a widespread English surname's assault on her exoticism, just as we could be meant to see and hear in the "Jones" an echo of the "Jonas" that Sternberg once was before changing his name to "Josef." (Having taken Ned's surname upon marrying him, Dietrich's character could then be interpreted as having taken the director's name upon her return to the stage—albeit not as his wife, but as Sternberg himself.) Yet to read too much into any of these names is to miss how they all fail to stick. As an instrument of capture, the name flounders; as an act of homage to beauty's *je ne sais quoi*, it proliferates.

By calling Dietrich's character both "Helen" and "Venus," the film is even more overt than its predecessors in linking Dietrich with the mythologemes of feminine beauty. It is an antiquity filtered, however, through Zola's *Nana* (1880), which Sternberg had initially planned to bring to the screen after completing *Shanghai Express*. Anxious that Dietrich was at risk of being rendered unusable for other types of roles, Paramount executives opposed this project yet nonetheless proved unable to deter Sternberg from any borrowings from Zola's novel about a courtesan. In *Nana* a woman who cannot sing is cast in the title role of *La Blonde Vénus* for which Offenbach's operetta *La Belle Hélène* (1864) served Zola as model. Yet

Dietrich's Helen as the blonde Venus, with the literariness of the allusion to Zola's Nana, enjoys wiggle room in relation to the figure of the prostitute: the distancing from the myth of woman that Zola wrings from his description of the papier-mâché Olympus of *La Blonde Vénus* is replicated with regard to the realism that deals with women's commercial degradation.

Blonde Venus is, in certain respects, also a reflection on the cinematic work of myth-making. The film does not call for a demolition of myth, but neither does it consume itself in its creation. It is as though by the time of their fifth collaboration Sternberg and Dietrich have enough trust in the durability of the Dietrich myth that they afford themselves a glimpse behind its façade, at the personal costs of being mythologized. The film stands as testament to Sternberg's empathy with his star *as star*. For Sternberg, there is no ordinary human being waiting to be brought gently out into the light from the oppressive shadow cast by the Dietrich myth. If Dietrich's character suffers, it is because her otherworldliness is not acknowledged. Other criteria for judging her conduct pertain. Ned Faraday casts Helen out and deprives her of access to her child because she has behaved contrary to his expectations (that she has had an affair with Nick Townsend is, unlike Captain Harvey's case in *Shanghai Express*, not just a matter of a hurried inference from appearances). Although he has the federal government and the prevailing morality on his side, he is in the wrong as far as the film is concerned: he has not come to terms with what it means to live with a mythical being.

Blonde Venus does not excuse Ned for failing to recognize the mythical nature of his wife even as the film dwells on the gimcrack, ramshackle, and sordid aspects of the Depression-era entertainment industry. The essence of the mythical is not incompatible with the insalubrious surroundings in which Helen finds herself. Opulence, dignity, and proficiency do not define it. What sets it apart is the suspension of norms and laws it introduces. Dietrich's character, who at the start of the film's history of events emerges naked from the waters like Venus and who is then carried off to a foreign land like Helen, brings to the nightclub stage an otherworldliness that has less to do with the supernatural than with the theater's intrinsic and bare exceptionalism. By putting in abeyance the reality that encompasses it, the stage throws open the doors to unearthly powers and to revolutionary futures while also, through its jealousy of its own exceptionalism and the tenuousness of its sphere of make-believe, warding off their realization in the world beyond the footlights. The ontological specificity of the stage lies in this invitation and its retraction, in its spatialization of a politico-eschatological tease. Lest it submerge itself in any extra-theatrical content, the purist stage is reluctant to reveal more than its own power to interrupt the reality that surrounds it, to say "No" to it. A fully articulated and credible illusion, for all the clearness with which it would mark a divergence from the perceptual experience of the rest of the auditorium, risks eclipsing the theater as theater, sacrificing to an alternative reality the revelation of its raw power to suspend what is. The "Hot Voodoo" number with which Helen opens her career at O'Connor's nightclub, and in which Dietrich's shortcomings as a singer are, as it were, showcased, comprises an extended gag on this megalomania and minimalism of theatrical revelation.

In *Blonde Venus* what analogy there is between the stage's suspension of normality and promiscuity's disregard of social conventions thickens almost to the point of identity. When Helen is interviewed by the booking agent Ben Smith, she is not asked to prove that she can sing and dance:

> SMITH. Let's see what you got.
> HELEN. What I've got?
> SMITH. Let's see your legs.
> HELEN *plucking up her dress*. Is that enough?
> SMITH *stonily*. For the time being.

A desk stands between Dietrich and the camera and keeps her legs out of sight when at Smith's injunction she hoists her dress a few inches. The reserve with which Sternberg shoots the scene dodges the degradation of the casting couch without ignoring it altogether (given that the display of Dietrich's legs in *The Blue Angel* had made them world-famous, the motivating consideration here is not whether it is proper to display them at all but rather whether in this setting, where Dietrich's character is alone in a stranger's office and financially dependent on his goodwill, display would amount to no more than objectification). Helen gives no sign of having expected a different type of audition, and she knows the value of what she has to offer. Smith's half-hearted efforts to feign nonchalance in the face of her physical charms soon give way to the admission: "You've certainly got me all hopped up, baby." Arriving at his office just as he plans to leave, Helen is told that everyone in the waiting room is ahead of her, but as an extradiegetic spotlight flagrantly singles her out among them, Smith is diverted into according her preferential treatment. The sexual appeal of Dietrich's character is inseparable from the cinematic medium: it is not left to make its case on its own. The experience of the conspicuousness of the beautiful is rendered concrete in the illumination that bathes Dietrich to the exclusion of her fellow cast members. In the way that Sternberg frames Dietrich, in the way that she is lit, her amoral physicality already merges with show business. Beauty as appearance is intrinsically an affair of spectacle. It lacks (or exceeds) the materiality of a good that can be bought or sold, and which a husband can pretend to own.

Having renounced her former profession upon marrying Ned, Helen commits herself without any noticeable disinclination to the duties, customs, and affections of being a wife and mother. And yet she seizes on the opportunity to return to the stage when she learns of the financial predicament resulting from Ned's illness. The couple broaches the topic with Helen in an apron and seated at a loom (the disconcertingly vampish diagonals of her penciled eyebrows prevent her from passing for a hieroglyph of domesticity). Ned is adamant that the high cost of his treatment does not justify Helen resuming her former occupation. At this rebuff to her proposal, notwithstanding the solicitude for his well-being in which she had wrapped it, Helen gets to her feet and standing behind Ned with her hands in the pockets of her apron she remarks airily: "I was going back to my old work anyway."

Although in its publicity blitz for *Blonde Venus* Paramount stressed the film's novelty in casting Dietrich in the role of an American housewife, there is an unmistakable relaxation in Dietrich's manner once she is back in a nightclub dressing room. The clarinet-heavy jazz processional to which Shanghai Lily enters Shanghai railway station is reprised, announcing the reassertion of the Dietrich persona that is larger than any one film. Seated in front of a mirror and applying her pancake makeup, Helen turns without a word of acknowledgment to examine Taxi Belle Hooper (Rita La Roy) who has barged into the dressing room they are to share. Even though it is her first appearance in the nightclub that Taxi claims to have helped put "on the map," Helen comports herself as the proprietor of a domain in which Taxi is at best a tolerated interloper. Her approach to the civilities of introduction is wholly uncollegial:

TAXI. My name's Taxi Belle Hooper. Taxi for short.
HELEN *looking at her reflection while adding mascara and smiling.* Do you charge for
   the first mile?
TAXI. Say, you trying to ride me?

The genuine tenderness of physical intimacy that Helen earlier exhibits in her interactions with her son is replaced here by a mordant pleasure in the wit with which she bullies Taxi. This is a facet of Helen's personality for which we are unprepared, except insofar as we allow the sassiness of Dietrich's previous performances to inform our reception of the role. Taxi, who was already irritable when she arrived and who quickly overlooks the slight to boast to Helen of the fifteen-hundred-dollar bracelet that she received from Nick Townsend, can dispense with the audience's sympathy. The rudeness that would have gained Helen an enemy in a different environment here merely serves to break the ice. Taxi feels no embarrassment in coming across as a rough-and-tumble gold digger. And from the interest she takes in Taxi's stories of Nick Townsend's generosity it is clear that Helen is sizing up her chances of reproducing her success, for the value of the bracelet just happens to be the price of Ned's medical treatment in Germany.

FIGURE 2.1. "Do you charge for the first mile?": Dietrich as Helen Jones, formerly Faraday puts on her makeup by the light of the malicious twinkle in her own eye in *Blonde Venus* (dir. Josef von Sternberg, Paramount Pictures, 1932).

The "Hot Voodoo" number that constitutes the heart of the next scene is one of the more dazzling flights of fancy in Sternberg and Dietrich's seven films together. The semiotic density of the sequence defies attempts to offer anything beyond the most rudimentary parsing. To pounding drums and a jazz band accompaniment, a gorilla with liquid streaming from its nostrils is led out on a chain by a line of twelve barefoot women in African-themed costumes and black Afro wigs, carrying painted shields and spears. When a patron asks the bartender (an uncredited Clarence Muse) if the gorilla is real, he gruffly denies it: "Say, lady, if that animal was real, I wouldn't be here!" But since he does so in a stutter, the begrudgingly offered reassurance—after all, it should hardly need pointing out that no licensed premises would let an animal of a gorilla's known strength and impetuosity wander among its clientele—is rendered ambiguous, at least for an audience that a lazy Hollywood directorial shorthand has trained to interpret stuttering as a sign of fear.[3] *Blonde Venus* opens up an ironic distance from the trope, familiar from reaction shots of characters (the white heterosexual adult male hero excepted) at their first sighting of something monstrous. All is not as it seems: the illusion is not to be pegged too easily. It is over two minutes into the routine before Dietrich, following an applause-cuing crescendo in the vigorous and inventive music by Ralph Rainger, reveals herself from inside the gorilla costume in a previously unseen outfit of ostrich feathers and diamantes (the sequence thus contrasts with Dietrich's first number in *Morocco* where the discrepancy between the dressing room and the performance proper is played down). The extended build-up heightens the stakes of the intended *coup de théâtre*. Donning a blonde Afro wig transpierced by golden arrows, Dietrich sings Sam Coslow's risqué lyrics for "Hot Voodoo," which end with the declaration: "I want to be bad!" (only two years earlier Paramount had released *Follow Thru* in which Zelma O'Neal performs on a night-club stage Ray Henderson, Lew Brown, and Buddy G. DeSylva's "I Want to Be Bad"). Dietrich's limited vocal range, projection, and technique, the relative woodenness with which she bounces from hip to hip while singing, her comically odd scooping on the rhymes "slave"/"cave" and "sensation"/"vacation" as well as the dowdy eroti-cism of her facial expressions are not such as to be able to capitalize on the dramatic tension of the earlier "big reveal"—when it comes, the song itself as performed by Dietrich is a bit of a wind egg. Although Sianne Ngai has argued that the sequence amounts to a cultural appropriation of Josephine Baker's nightclub act, the theft is all too openly bungled for this to be the sum of what is going on: Dietrich cannot be considered competition for Baker on the latter's own terrain.[4] When the song ends, the audience claps politely, but without any extraordinary enthusiasm.

And yet "Hot Voodoo" is a mesmerizing moment in Hollywood cinema. Dietrich's performance is not set up for ridicule, even as it fails to meet prevailing standards of voice production. For Sternberg, Dietrich was never simply someone who could not sing. In the early drafts of *The Blue Angel*, Rosa Fröhlich, the precursor of Dietrich's Lola Lola, suffers bitterly from the lack of appreciation of her meager vocal talents.[5] That the finished film adopted a different course is consistent with certain funda-mental tenets of Sternberg's artistic practice. He is indifferent to the cinema's ca-pacity for showing the world and the people in it to be worse than initially thought.[6] At issue in this indifference is not a beautiful soul's discomfort with unseemliness and contradiction: Sternberg's films scarcely shy away from conflict, insanity, turpi-tude, and disorder. He is no cynic. *Underworld* (1927), for example, notwithstanding the influence it was to exert on the gangster genre, shares nothing of the jaundiced view of human nature that was to typify film noir: the suspicions regarding Feathers McCoy (Evelyn Brent) and Rolls Royce (Clive Brook) that torment Bull Weed (George Bancroft) as he waits on death row turn out to be unwarranted, for rather than run off together they risk their lives to save him. By declining in *The Blue Angel* to portray Dietrich as the butt of audience derision, Sternberg manifests not merely his solicitude for his star's public persona, but moreover his sense of pacing regarding the dramatic use of humiliation: because disgrace is not distributed, but apportioned exclusively to Professor Rat, there is no solidarity among sufferers on which he could count in order to resist his eventual madness and death. If Rat finally considers himself undeceived by Lola Lola, he cannot blame appearances for having led him astray: nothing in her character was hidden from him. The cinema has not punctured a specious illusion of its own making. In *The Last Command*, Sergius (Emil Jannings) dies, by contrast, convinced of the cinematic illusion of a recreated Russia. For Sternberg, the fakery intrinsic to this industrial art form can be inflected and refashioned, but cinema cannot throw it aside altogether without erasing itself just as, in *Blonde Venus*, for all her collisions with fate Dietrich's character never gives over the poetry of appearance for the prose of what is.

Vulnerability here is not destructive of the burnished image of the star. In the "Hot Voodoo" number the "big reveal" is not that O'Connor's new act can barely "croon in a pinch" (no one in the nightclub audience laughs at Helen Jones), but rather that show business can get by with a tiny displacement from the everyday world as we know it. The Blonde Venus is both the reality behind the illusion of the gorilla suit and the spectacle toward which the cinema and the theater ascend. The truth of show business that Helen Jones asserts in her person is that of a bare will to difference from the surrounding environment. There is disruption without a subsequent congealing into an alternative content and substance. As a revelation, this is as enigmatic in its own way and as subtle as that which the Hasidic tale recorded by Ernst Bloch, among others, discerns in the coming of the Messiah:

> Another rabbi, a true Kabbalist, once said: To bring about the kingdom of freedom, it is not necessary that everything be destroyed, and a new world begun; rather, this cup, or that bush, or that stone, and so all things must only be shifted a little. Because this "a little" is hard to do, and its measure so hard to find, humanity cannot do it in this world; instead this is why the Messiah comes.[7]

Show business, in maintaining—more precisely, in attaining—its small displacement, anticipates and forestalls the coming of the Messiah: it is the anti-Messianism that is the true Messiah. On its own this is nonetheless not enough to differentiate it from Christianity, which in accepting the execution of Christ stood Jewish Messianism on its head. Something else is needed. Jorge Luis Borges touches on the uncanny resemblance between Christianity's anti-Messianism and art: "This imminence of a revelation which does not occur is, perhaps, the aesthetic phenomenon."[8] Insofar as the aesthetic domain promises without following through on its promise, what it promises is disappointment. Helen's pleasure is the antirealist and irreligious pleasure of knowingly occupying a space that is neither of this world nor of the world to come—the space of mere appearance. The sobriety with which she inhabits this space does not preclude pleasure even as it prepares for disappointment. The tangible and infectious pleasure that Helen draws from performing differs from the physiological rush of the singer who, from faith in art's promise, strains his or her body to the utmost in the act of producing sound.

Even as a gorilla, Helen is not in exile on the stage. O'Connor's nightclub burgeons with tropical vegetation. Monstera, cactus, and fern rim the stage and band, a painted drop curtain mimics dense jungle, and branches whose trunks are never seen reach down from above over the patrons. In nearly every shot of the sequence Sternberg ensures that greenery intrudes into view, at times constituting a dark herbaceous border that crowds and offsets the image at the center of the shot (customers' out-of-focus heads then assume this function in the shot of Taxi at the bar). The clutter that is emblematic of the Sternbergian frame is the director's countermeasure in response to the camera's flattening of space into a two-dimensional image. If the space of the image is not to be the dead space that Sternberg deplored, the invisible friction and resistance confronted by the body moving in concrete space must be rendered visible in some way. The intrusiveness of design in Sternberg's films thus translates Newtonian law for the weightless bodies of the cinematic image, and while it does not give these bodies weight as such, it can instill within the frame the interplay of forces of a specifically visual gravity.

Notwithstanding the outlandishness and theatricality of the "Hot Voodoo" number, it does not stand apart from the film as a whole and its action. Having been alerted to the munificence of Cary Grant's character, Helen's gorilla throws him a targeted look as she ascends the stairs leading up to the stage. Although it lacks the manic fervor of the stare with which King Kong first espies Fay Wray a year later, Helen's glance is nonetheless the opening move in the relationship that she and Nick Townsend are to develop (that "Hot Voodoo" references the choreography and bobbing feathers of the backup dancers in Lola Lola's cautionary "Blonde Women" from *The Blue Angel* is an intertextual admonition that, as befits a tragic hero caught up in his own story, is lost on Nick Townsend). A neglect of this glance from Helen is the enabling condition of Peter Baxter's reading of the scene in *Just Watch!: Sternberg, Paramount and America*:

> The 'Hot Voodoo' number rigidly excludes any suggestion of the woman's subjective perception from the stage. The only diegetic point of view that matters is Nick's, and the long dolly-in is a key instrument for allying the experience of the film-spectator with that of Nick in the nightclub audience. In its movement it inscribes the sequence with the sense of the physical distance that lies between the subject and 'the absolute object of desire.'[9]

Nick, as an audience member, may believe that staring is his prerogative, but concealed within the hunter's hide she fabricated from a gorilla costume Helen has already taken his measure. Helen's agency, personality, and interests are not occluded by the gorilla costume. Her deliverance from the costume is thus no rescue of beauty from the beast, just as her artless rendition of the song fails to confirm the putative distance of white civilization from a mythical African savagery.

Billed as the blonde Venus, Helen does not stand forth as her ostensibly true self at the moment of the "big reveal," since by immediately putting on the blonde Afro wig she, in effect, defers to its hair color as the basis for her stage name. When Helen is on the run with her son Johnny, she catches sight of a photo of herself in the newspaper wearing this wig. The choice of photo is ludicrous given that the article's explicit purpose is to garner information from the newspaper's readership concerning Helen's whereabouts. It is a feature of her act neither in the Star Café in Baltimore where she subsequently performs "You Little So-And-So" nor in the Paris nightclub where she sings "I Couldn't Be Annoyed." Ned, who initiates the police search for Helen, presumably could have provided a more representative photo, one more in keeping with Helen's everyday appearance. But then as far as Ned is concerned, it is not Helen-as-housewife who is on the run. The woman who has abducted his son is a cabaret entertainer who, thanks to a giant wig with golden arrows stuck in it, barely resembles the woman with whom he had been living as husband and wife.

The blonde Venus who emerges from a sea of fur on the stage of O'Connor's nightclub is a confection of limelight and feathers, deftly patched together from crimped hair, greasepaint, and sequins. It is one phase in the work to which Helen returns in defiance of the man she married. Given that Helen bears the name of "The Blonde Venus" only in this section of the film, the "Hot Voodoo" number becomes, as it were, the film's title track, a crystallization of its handling of the mythological. The mythologization of Dietrich's character is accordingly inseparable from her commercialization. Diegetically and extradiegetically, the choice of Helen's stage name and the film's title is a matter of marketing imperatives rather than an acknowledgment of a supernatural visitation: O'Connor confers on Helen the name of "The Blonde Venus" in a last-minute advertising ploy just as Paramount used the film's title to build on its earlier promotion of Dietrich as a "screen goddess." The mythical being that in *Blonde Venus* Sternberg figuratively draws down to earth literally has to climb out of a gorilla costume.

In the broadness of its humor, it is a moment of mythological revelation conspicuously at variance with the star persona that Dietrich was zealously to guard in the decades after her collaboration with Sternberg. This is not to suggest that Dietrich became a victim of her own myth and a slave to the maintenance of its poise and decorum. As different as the myth of O'Connor's blonde Venus is from the myth of Dietrich as postwar concert artist and living monument to both Golden-Age Hollywood and Sternberg's stylization of her, the two share a certain lightness of touch.

The freedom with which the later Dietrich cohabited with her own myth becomes, for Silvia Bovenschen, emblematic of a kind of sovereignty in the handling of the patriarchal image of femininity. Recalling the 1973 BBC/CBS television special *An Evening with Marlene Dietrich*, Bovenschen describes a performer who, unlike Helen Jones, is not about to be drowned out by her own orchestra:

> An artistic product came on stage, every movement perfected, every gesture precisely rehearsed, premeditated, every facial expression calculated for aesthetic effect. Every movement of her head or hands—all these were spare, artificial. Added up, the details gave the impression that decades of experience lead to precision. Although she cannot really sing, the audience went wild over the familiar old songs. In performance she was totally cool, faintly ironic, and even when she was portraying emotion everything was staged, she made no attempt to make the emotion appear genuine. When she sings—actually it is more like talking than singing—she slurs, softens the refrains, but even this is not fortuitous. The pose is intentional, it says, you know this one already, I know you will be pleased if I sing it. [. . .] Behind her is an early picture of herself, only the head. Her face is older now, but even this change seems not so much the result of the biological aging process; it seems much more something artificially arranged, a sort of displacement intended to signify historical distance. And her body is just as artificial, absolutely smooth as though encased in some unfamiliar fabric—we are watching a woman demonstrate the representation of a woman's body. [. . .] The myth appears on stage and consciously demonstrates itself as myth. Just like in the zoo: the monkey is suddenly the observer, and the people are the ones standing and staring out from behind bars. [. . .] Whereas before an actress had to satisfy the expectations of the audience, now the audience must conform to hers. The myth is on the receiving end and consumes the audience. She gazes down from the stage not once but twice, once as an image and once as an artist.[10]

As Elfriede Jelinek was to write later in her obituary for Dietrich, it becomes unclear who is to count as the audience.[11] Inasmuch as the gaze is a property of Dietrich's public image (of her "brand"), her appearance can no more be fully reified than an icon (whether an icon can be stripped of all religion and remain an icon on the strength of its returning gaze alone is a separate and, admittedly, not particularly knotty question). The eternal "now" of myth subsists henceforth only as a performance style. The precision of Dietrich's performance, as Bovenschen observes, has less to do with an involuntary repetition of the past than with a playing, so to speak, with control itself. Dietrich's precision does not aim at the perfect reproduction of her performances in the films that made her famous (even a casual comparison will not fail to spot the differences). Instead, what is arguably at stake is a reinvention of these numbers so that when performed in isolation they do not have to forego any of that irony and detachment which Dietrich's interpretations from the 1930s owe to the larger filmic structures in which they first appeared. Dietrich neither repudiates Sternberg's image of her nor condemns herself to a futile attempt to re-enact it for a live audience. It is as though she translates the indelibility of the cinematic image (rather than its actual content) into a self-consciously iterable performance style. Cabaret here comes upon its own equivalent of the Japanese tea ceremony. Hand movements become more disciplined, glances more calculated as the characterological complexity that Sternberg would take an entire film to set out is concentrated in a single song. If the world-weariness of the Dietrich persona that Dietrich constructed for herself—and that is at once a detachment from her own myth and a component of it—little resembles Helen's exuberance during "Hot Voodoo," it is an affective rendering of that same displacement and opening-up which Sternberg and Dietrich achieve through their "big reveal" and its pastiche on revelation. Dietrich, who was to sing the same songs over and over again during her long concert career, devised for herself a knowingly dispassionate method of presentation that secured for her the distance that, by contrast, the character of Helen Jones could count on as a given in the absence of rehearsals and reprises of "Hot Voodoo." Having performed the number only once, Helen Jones can slip away from it uncompromised and undefined by it: as the German proverb has it, *einmal ist keinmal* [just the once is not at all]. The distance that Sternberg puts between a mythical being and everyday concerns and vulnerabilities is, for the postwar Dietrich, not enough: there has to be an additional step back from this very distance.

In one respect, cinema automatically has access to the dimension of myth. For Sternberg, the filmmaker's task is not how to attain this access, but rather how to manage and to curb it. The eternal "now" of myth irrupts into the image during the process of technological recording. The powers of history and biological decay are banished beyond the edges of the frame while an otherwise transient act or state of affairs acquires the immutability of ritual. This technological transformation of the profilmic floods the atemporal realm of mythology with phenomena whose presence there is not underwritten by the usual cultural and psychosomatic mechanisms. So long as the footage survives in one form or another and there is an audience to view it, the insignificant cheats the oblivion that was once guaranteed it. Inasmuch as the camera can mythologize anything, Sternberg's undertaking in relation to Dietrich is not simply to bestow on her the timelessness of a mythical being. In the case of *Blonde Venus*, he sets three modes of the eternal "now" in dialogue with one another: the iterability at the heart of show business as an ongoing financial concern gestures toward and caricatures the eternal "now" of myth, just as cinema's technological fixing of time outstrips the theater's own efforts yet shows up only itself in the ease of its accomplishment (the inhuman automatism of photographic recording injects its own loss and alienation of human agency into the arresting of the passage of time). Dietrich's character, who is introduced as an actress but who then makes a living as a cabaret entertainer, is a being with no exact place within show business. The latter is a refuge, a relic, and a parody of the mythological realm in an irreligious society: the iterability of a cabaret routine such as "Hot Voodoo" with its invasion of the reality inside the nightclub is what remains of ritual after the definitive withdrawal of the gods, even as the zaniness of the routine might be thought to guard against any reactivation of the sacred.

Dietrich is the blonde Venus who has to perform her acts only the once. What repetition there is lies with the multiple screenings of the film and any unused takes. Although *Blonde Venus* ventures behind the scenes of show business, it ignores iteration as a constitutive feature of the industry. The viewer is spared the spectacle of repetitive theatrical labor wherein a cabaret entertainer starts to resemble a factory employee on a production line. (Dietrich in her postwar concert career refused to conceal from her audience the exertion involved in performing and hence in effect demythologizes her own myth at the very moment of constructing it.) Helen speaks of her "work," although by occluding the repetitive aspect of show business that has it converge with more familiar forms of labor, the film declines to distract from the aura of prostitution (sex work) that hovers around her. "Hot Voodoo" comes to appear an elaborate means to solicit the attentions of Nick Townsend, the giver of lifesaving fifteen-hundred-dollar bracelets. The blonde Venus has to perform her act only the once because its purpose, as far as the film is concerned, is fulfilled as soon as Nick is sufficiently interested to ask to visit her in her dressing room. This is not the singularity of the deed performed in a heroic, god-crowded past to be then repeatedly re-enacted in ritual. Rather, it is the singularity of a cinematic storytelling that, while envying the theater its spectacle and artifice, wants nothing of its nontechnological iterations.

When Nick first sets eyes on Helen, she is at her furthest remove from the everyday. In the study in which he contributed significantly to the restoration of

Sternberg's standing as a director in the 1960s, Andrew Sarris queries the casting of Cary Grant in the role of Nick Townsend opposite Dietrich's Helen:

> The gangster is played by a still callow Cary Grant, whose pairing with Dietrich is not very memorable. Yet it is doubtful that Grant and Dietrich would ever have worked as a satisfactory team. For all its smooth grace, Grant's style is essentially realistic. He is a real person, not next door necessarily, but somewhere. Dietrich is a fantasy figure from nowhere, and no actress can play properly with Grant without some sort of address. By the same token, Grant would only intrude on Dietrich's style of perpetual mystery with the demystifying lurch of his probing personality. That is why Grant is so superbly cast in Hitchcock's films: he supplies the proper note of reality Hitchcock requires to orchestrate his suspense.[12]

Because Dietrich and Grant do not remain together at the end of the film, it is not dramatically necessary for the two of them to work satisfactorily as a team. And given that Grant's Townsend is only one of a succession of men in Sternberg's films who form less-than-convincing romantic partnerships with Dietrich's characters, it is hard to allege a desire for on-screen chemistry was frustrated by the casting of Grant in the role. But there is a third criticism in Sarris's remarks: it bears on the perceived damage to "Dietrich's style of perpetual mystery" from the casting of an actor with Grant's "probing personality." All his ministrations to the cinematic genesis of Dietrich's mystery aside, Sternberg himself does not always handle his star with kid gloves as far as how she is depicted. Although this can be put down to his ambivalence toward her, the effect is to establish a dialectics (or auto-contestation of hagiography) within the canonical image of Dietrich's mystery. In *Blonde Venus*, among the series of indignities and disorientations to which the film subjects its central character and whereby it puts Dietrich's mystery to the test, Grant's "probing personality" is not an obvious candidate for inclusion. Given that Helen frankly admits to Nick at the outset the mercenary nature of her interest in him, the secret that Grant's quizzical persona could be said later to unearth—namely, that her motivations in her dealings with him are *not* merely financial—does not debase her.

By means of her performance of "Hot Voodoo," Helen acquires both the money to send her husband away for six months to Germany and the freedom to initiate a relationship with Nick. Cinematographically, Sternberg abstains from condemning Helen for her marital infidelity. By delegating to her husband and the retributions in the plot the upholding of the moral standpoint for whose promulgation the Motion Picture Producers and Distributors of America (MPPDA) had their own political and economic reasons, Sternberg gives himself the room in the *mise-en-scène* to declare his solidarity with Helen: she is not in the wrong for engaging in an extra-marital affair.

For Lea Jacobs, in her monograph on Hollywood's fallen woman genre, the script itself of *Blonde Venus* is a complex balancing act of concessions and provocations:

> The idiosyncrasies of a director like Sternberg flourished as much *because of* as *despite* the constraints imposed on representation within the studio system. *Blonde Venus* could go as far as it did in aligning the maternal and the sexually deviant because Sternberg went to great lengths to accommodate the Studio Relations Committee in the treatment of detail. The film is in many ways the logical extension of a system which favored the development of indirect or allusive forms of representation.[13]

The scenes between Helen and Johnny become, in Jacobs' assessment, a bargaining chip:

> I will argue that the emphasis on motherhood in and of itself provided a way of managing or controlling what the MPPDA considered the potentially offensive aspects of female deviance. From the point of view of the Studio Relations Committee, the concept of motherhood had a real strategic value; it provided the cornerstone of a moralizing and highly normative discourse which defined the woman's place in terms of her function within the domestic sphere.[14]

Blonde Venus not only takes advantage of the naïve assumption that maternal feeling and promiscuity cannot coexist, it also critiques it in a rethinking of the sexual morality governing the family unit in 1930s America. At its conclusion nothing confirms that the price of Helen's reconciliation with her husband is a renunciation of her lover.

Commenting on *Angel* (1937), the lackluster Lubitsch film in which Dietrich, in the title role, again plays an alienated wife opposite Herbert Marshall, Molly Haskell analyzes the similarly unconventional terms on which the two finally are reunited (for all his hostility toward Sternberg, culminating in the machinations that ended the latter's career at Paramount, Lubitsch did not eschew the new moral terrain that his studio rival had broached in his collaborations with Dietrich):

> In the end, Marshall discovers that Angel is his wife and makes the choice that means he will take her back, forever—a gesture that would normally be read as her redemption through his forgiveness, but which is actually the contrary. For

it is his acceptance of a side of her that he may not ever be able to fulfill that is *his* redemption.[15]

Ned's redemption in *Blonde Venus*, to the extent that it can be inferred from the film's ambiguous final tableau, involves his unconditional acceptance of how Helen behaves: that he does not forgive her, rather than being an expression of his intransigent anger, is because he sees that she has done nothing for him to forgive. They who have both sold their bodies to outside parties will henceforth no longer admit a relationship to property as the foundation of their marriage.

If there is a critique of materialism in *Blonde Venus*, neither religion nor idealism inspires it. Materialism founders in Sternberg's films on the unpossessability of mere appearance. Helen's beauty, which not coincidentally opens doors for her into show business, is the stuff of spectacle. It is irreducible to the objectivity of that which can be possessed. Inasmuch as we recognize the beautiful by means of our pleasure in the perception of it, the unattainability associated with the beautiful is also the intimacy with which it inhabits our perceptual apparatus, refusing to stand over against us as an object among objects classed and ordered by their properties. In the unease of its concourse with objects, beauty is its own myth even as it generates myth.

Given beauty's exceptionalism, Helen's forays into the bleaker regions of Depression-era America have an aspect of slumming to them. The film does not pretend otherwise. No sooner has she hit rock bottom than she rebounds. Having been tracked down by the authorities and having had her son torn from her, an inebriated Helen checks in at a flophouse offering "lodging for the night 15¢ for ladies only." She promptly offloads the fifteen-hundred dollars that her husband had forced upon her in discharging his "debt," staggers off through the dormitory's suspended hooks and lamps and clouds of cigarette smoke in search of "a better bed," and when she is next seen, she is decked out in a white tailcoat with glittering lapels as the principal attraction of a Paris revue. This is not the unshakeable misfortune that fastens on James Allen (Paul Muni) in Mervyn LeRoy's contemporaneous *I Am a Fugitive from a Chain Gang* with its exposé of pervasive injustice, brutality, and deceit in the U.S. correctional system. The somber picaresque of *Blonde Venus* skirts the widespread economic insecurity of the period, neither naming its causes nor allowing it to exercise its real-world dominance over the film's protagonist. This is, in one respect, the dishonesty of Hollywood.[16] In another respect, Sternberg mythologizes not in order to draw an ideological veil over the conditions of the proletariat's oppression, but rather in order to draw closer to the phenomenon that fascinates him, namely, Dietrich's free-floating beauty.

And I shall see
Some squeaking Cleopatra boy my greatness
I'th' posture of a whore.

SHAKESPEARE, *Antony and Cleopatra*, 5.2.218–20

3 *The Scarlet Empress*
HISTORY AS FARCE

The Scarlet Empress (1934) is the most comic of Sternberg and Dietrich's collaborations. With its paean to female sexuality and its bizarre sets, it profits from the oft-remarked freedom that dropped in Sternberg's lap during this period of organizational upheaval at Paramount.[1] But the film also seizes upon the license that Hollywood costume drama already had claimed for itself in the handling of history. If it goes further than previous examples of the genre in piling distortions upon inaccuracies and anachronisms, it is because it wishes to stake ownership of the comedy that results from botching the representation of the past. *The Scarlet Empress* is the satire on European despotism that lurked within the genre and that fell to European émigrés to draw out into the open. What in other hands was naiveté and a negligence regarding the facts becomes in their hands aggression and humor, an even utopian levity in the face of the stolid pieties of tradition and consolidated power. *The Scarlet Empress* is the joke on European despotism that they believed the political and economic conditions of America, at least as they experienced them, rendered possible for them to make. History is reprised as camp, and lavish spectacle, once the prerogative of tyranny and an instrument in its mystification, here denies that there is anything beyond appearances.

Sternberg is a filmmaker who places demands, as it were, on frivolousness. When he declared "the supreme value to me is justice," he was not only indulging his well-known fondness for the consternation of his interlocutors, but also—and more specifically—bucking against the widespread perception of his work as that of a mere entertainer.[2] In one respect, the provocativeness that Sternberg intends for his statement requires that he not be entitled to make it (after all, his studio-bound films, with their concerted fabrication of a star image, differ markedly from the social documentaries more commonly associated with the good that cinema is able to achieve). But in another respect, there is an ethics of superficiality that can be attributed to Sternberg's filmmaking and that his statement can be interpreted as affirming. The justice of a film such as *The Scarlet Empress*, what justice it has, is located on the surface and in the entertainment it provides.

Doing justice to the surface is one way to understand Joseph Conrad's famous statement of the mission of art: "Art itself may be defined as a single-minded attempt to render the highest kind of justice to the visible universe, by bringing to light the truth, manifold and one underlying its every aspect."[3] Art does justice to the surface by not passing beyond the visible universe to the metaphysical truths in the contemplation of which it would lose its difference from Platonism. It brings to light what is already there on the surface. If Conrad's vocation is not alien to Sternberg, it is because the surface is not a given and stands in need of its own revelation. In his last interview Sternberg repudiated the suggestion, which the interviewer had not in fact made, that there was any intellectual depth to his pictures.[4] This lack of depth, rather than being nothing more than the passively endured lot of a director who knows no better, is put to work in *The Scarlet Empress*. A figure from the history of European despotism is reimagined as a Hollywood star. By means of her personal appeal, Dietrich does not so much make sense of Catherine II's rise to power in mid-eighteenth-century Russia as parody it, transcribing it for the insubstantiality of the cinematic image.

There is, of course, no urgency in 1930s America to the choice of Catherine II in particular as an object of political satire: *The Scarlet Empress* does not bear comparison with Chaplin's *The Great Dictator* (1940) as a response to an immediate threat. (To judge by her daughter's account of the making of the film, as far as Dietrich was concerned, the Russian setting justified itself by the numbers of furs she could reasonably wear and for which she believed she could rely on Adolph Zukor, the founder of Paramount, as a one-time furrier to share her appreciation.) Far closer to hand as a catalyst for the film, among several costume dramas of the period dealing with female monarchs, is MGM's *Queen Christina* (1933), starring Greta Garbo and directed by Rouben Mamoulian with whom Dietrich worked on *The Song of Songs* from the same year.[5] Nevertheless, the butt of the humor of *The Scarlet Empress* is not merely the costume drama of Sternberg's more earnest contemporaries. The film aspires to capitalize on the absurdities of the genre rather than to invite their condemnation through caricaturing them. Instead of treating them as transgressions that call for a reassertion of historical responsibility, it treats them as cues for the opening out of a history other than the one that happened. Piggybacking on Hollywood's lack of historical sense, satire here applies itself to history as such. If the comedy of *The Scarlet Empress* is not the flip-side of the disappointed moralism that is often ascribed to satirists, it is because it is unclear that Sternberg has any interest in seeing through the outlandish fantasy that he has created. The American fantasy of a break with European history is embraced without being mistaken for reality. Everything in *The Scarlet Empress* is ludicrous, but that is presented as a reason for enjoying it rather than for rejecting it.

In the opening credits the film purports to be based on a diary by Catherine II. It is a gambit. That the composition of the script entailed nothing beyond the arrangement of excerpts attributed to Manuel Komroff is not a belief that the film itself reinforces. Dietrich's nine-year-old daughter, Maria Riva, plays Sophia Frederica, the future Catherine the Great, in the first scene. The testy interaction between her and her mother—delightfully played by Olive Tell, who was Dietrich's senior by only seven years—establishes the farcical tone of what is to follow. The young Sophia petulantly announces that she wants to be a "toe-dancer," a term that did not exist before the late nineteenth century and that refers to a ballet technique first adopted in the 1830s. When the doctor takes his leave to perform his ancillary duties as the public executioner, Sophia sets to wondering, with a pensively crooked finger to her lips, if she might someday become a hangman. Having earlier proclaimed to her mother that she had no desire to be a queen, Sophia finds that her curiosity is piqued on learning that Peter the Great, Ivan the Terrible, and other Russian tsars and tsarinas were hangmen. This initiates a fantasy sequence from Sophia's point of view: her face dissolves to a string of acts of brutality, centering on a Grand Guignol vision of a frock-coated Peter the Great wielding an axe in quick succession on previously prepared victims. As a foreshadowing of Sophia's later temperament, it might seem that it is immediately retracted, for in the next scene Sophia, now played by Dietrich, is a perpetually open-mouthed ingénue.[6] Yet the visual segue between the fantasy sequence and Dietrich's first scene is the close correspondence between the back-and-forth movement of a man suspended upside down within a giant bell and Sophia's motion and place within the overlapping shot as five young gentlewomen take turns to push her on a rose-entwined swing in her family's garden: the ruling class's show of harmlessness is not to be given much credence.

Cast in these early scenes as an unworldly teenager, the thirty-three-year-old Dietrich also must contend with audiences' familiarity with her prior roles as a nightclub entertainer, a spy, and a courtesan. The gap between her person and her role, which is there in her previous films because of her "transcendental" approach to acting, is expanded and exploited for comic effect.[7] A random assortment of material artifacts from different decades and centuries tumble into the ostensibly eighteenth-century setting. Dietrich, who stands apart from her milieu in her preceding films for Sternberg, is now still more of a stranger to the world around her. History, without having its cruelties airbrushed out of the picture, is thereby presented as the stuff of farce. Dietrich's unplaceableness has become an outright burlesque on the realist pretensions of Hollywood costume drama. A paradigmatic use of age-inappropriate casting to fracture the realism within which a filmic world might otherwise congeal is Randal Kleiser's *Grease* (1978). To weaken the hold of realism over an audience's reception of a film is to prepare the way for a scene to open out into a nondiegetic musical number. The lengthened vowel sounds and up-beat delivery with which Hollywood actors were often wont to nudge the threshold of song, flirting with the passage across it, plant the nondiegetic musical number as an immanent possibility of a scene, as though the truth of mid-twentieth-century American optimism is to be found in the genre's need for an anacrusis and not in a psychological attitude. Dietrich, whose big musical numbers take place on stage accompanied by an orchestra and whose singing voice does not differ significantly from her speaking voice, is not an advertisement for the art of the transition. The antirealist pressure she applies to the role of the youthful Catherine the Great has the effect of cracking it open for the sake of an eventual revelation of Dietrich herself (the star as song).

As Sybil DelGaudio notes, the historicist aspirations of *The Scarlet Empress*, pliable as they are concerning the design choices for the supporting cast, are relaxed even further with respect to Dietrich's hair and wardrobe:

> Even with stylization an apparent consideration, however, the presentation of the star and contemporary standards of beauty and style are still carefully regarded. Early in the film Dietrich's hair, unlike the hairstyle of the other women in the film, is not arranged in the eighteenth-century Madame Pompadour style, but rather in an acceptably contemporary shoulder-length style with side curls and bangs that flatter and frame Dietrich's angular face. [. . .] In contrast to the other women of the court, she wears costumes of chiffon and other diaphanous fabrics that do not gibe with the historical accounts of the wide use of brocades and other heavy fabrics. Dietrich's accessories are also often historically and geographically incorrect, as it is unlikely that feathers appeared in the frigid Russian climate as frequently as they did as trim for Dietrich's costumes.[8]

The task with which Sternberg charges Dietrich—and for the execution of which the resources of Paramount are at her disposal—is to stand out. Whereas in *Shanghai Express* prostitution is the ploy by means of which Dietrich catches the eye, in *The Scarlet Empress* the anachronisms that differentiate her from her fellow cast members have a comparable outcome. The incompleteness of the invocation of the past in *The Scarlet Empress* means that individual citations of the eighteenth century, shot against the backdrop of a freshly constructed set or juxtaposed with Dietrich's 1930s glamor, call attention to themselves.[9] They obtain thereby a jaggedness that is the counterpart, in a different register, of Peter Ballbusch's crude sculptures of tortured and morose human figures that crowd Sternberg's Russian court.

This incoherence and anarchy of the design of *The Scarlet Empress* is what constitutes the film's signature style. The design compromises that afflict the realist ambitions of a low-budget period drama and are a source of unintended comedy are taken up as artistic devices. A cheap-looking diorama stands in for an establishing shot of a Russian cityscape and clashes with the opulence of the court sets (not that authenticity, as a value in the case for outdoor location shoots, has much hold on Sternberg's practice as a filmmaker). The accumulation of incongruities, by frustrating the emergence of a stable world, calls into doubt the norms, whether social or technical, with which a character's actions might be deemed in agreement. Far more is up in the air than in a comedy of manners and far more is askew. Its theatrical precedents are not to be met with in the observational humor of the English stage. As it plays havoc with the world that it makes an ambivalent show of depicting, it harks back to the *Posse* of nineteenth-century German-language dramatists such as Christian Grabbe and Johann Nestroy. But equivalents and inspirations are much closer to hand in the free-for-all of the comedies the Marx Brothers made at Paramount in the early thirties—in some respects, *The Scarlet Empress* comes across as a lingering trace of the brothers after their departure for MGM.

In the film the arbitrariness of the exercise of power under despotism converges with the capriciousness of farce. It is an environment that is at once ridiculous and terrifying. In the absence of the rule of law there is not even a prevailing sense of decorum to regulate conduct at the imperial court. Sophia Frederica, on whom the Empress Elizabeth (Louise Dresser) decides to bestow the "good Russian name" of "Catherine," is introduced to this milieu without there being any suggestion that she will put it to rights. Dubbing her in the title sequence "the ill-famed Messalina of the North," the film charts her metamorphosis from a Prussian innocent abroad to an adept in a Machiavellian promiscuity. *The Scarlet Empress* does not censure Catherine for coming to occupy the site of despotic license. Yet Sternberg has not overseen an apology for autocratic government. The despot's freedom of action at which Dietrich's Catherine arrives is purely cinematic: it does not exist beyond the frame because it cannot be disentangled from Dietrich's appearance as lit and shot by Sternberg and Bert Glennon.

What remains of despotism in *The Scarlet Empress* is beauty. While *The Devil Is a Woman* is at times a rancorous reflection on the despotism specific to beauty, the earlier film not only endeavors to explain Catherine's rise to power by means of her beauty, but also even to substitute beauty for despotism. The sovereign's immunity from prosecution under his or her own laws becomes the classificatory irrelevance of rules to a beauty that is like no other. For Sternberg, diverging from a long tradition, the uncanny double of the despot who flouts the law in pursuit of self-interest is not the just ruler who disregards the letter of the law for the sake of the justice that is its spirit. Sternberg doubles the despot with Dietrich. She does not repurpose the despot's extralegal freedom of action with an eye to the unlegislatable justice of Aristotle's ἐπιείκεια (equity).[10] The political exceptionalism that Catherine makes her own is identical with her appearance. Justice, which in the public's eyes legitimizes the unbound ruler's freedom of action, is here replaced by beauty: the sacral glow of Locke's "God-like Prince" survives in the electrical illumination with which Sternberg bathes Dietrich.[11]

As perverse and reprehensibly flippant as this substitution of the physical for the ethical no doubt is, it is not an idiosyncrasy on Sternberg's part. Hollywood costume dramas on the lives of crowned heads of state, inasmuch as they are star vehicles, are predisposed to reconfiguring the political status of their subjects as an affair of physical presence, as though such a translation is necessary for the monarch's exceptionalism to make sense to an audience in a republic. The result is ambiguous. On the one hand, monarchy is overlaid with an allure foreign to it, whereby it generates an attraction it rarely gratifies, and, on the other hand, it pre-empts and wards off the case for a restoration of monarchy by denying that there is anything to it beyond the looks and charm that republics are perfectly well able to accommodate (the nostalgia, in short, is misdirected). In *The Scarlet Empress*, the treatment of monarchy is admittedly more fervid. While Dietrich's Catherine in her rise to power is not a comic figure of contempt, the film takes pains with its fairy-tale sets and psychological implausibilities to disabuse its audience of the belief that it represents the reality of existence under a monarch: Sternberg's Catherine the Great is the false memory of despotism designed to block a resurgence of the real thing—that is one work of justice that beauty can here be said to perform.

With its conversion of autocracy into beauty, *The Scarlet Empress* recapitulates a centuries-long development in aesthetic history concerning the allowance made for rule-deviation. Although the eighteenth century does not invent the idea that there is a beauty that cannot be accounted for by means of a conformity to a class, it displays a pronounced interest in the phenomenon.[12] The objective rules by means of which we consider ourselves able to recognize the beautiful, differentiating it from the ugly and the aesthetically indifferent because it agrees with the model of its respective class of entities, manifests mathematically perfect proportions, and so forth, do not adequately cover everything that we experience to be beautiful. Something escapes. That to which Bouhours, Leibniz, and others refer as the *"je ne sais quoi"* of beauty becomes by the end of the century the focus of Kant's analysis of free beauty (*pulchritudo vaga*) in the *Critique of Judgement*. Kant's delineation of free beauty contributed in no small degree to the consolidation of the transition in taste and artistic practice from neoclassicism to romanticism. The anomalous and the eccentric entered upon their inheritance. Under the influence of a widespread misreading of what the third *Critique* understands by pure aesthetic judgment, the beauty that by virtue of its resistance to cognitive judgment had piqued Kant's curiosity as a philosophical problem soon constituted for Baudelaire the truth or essence of beauty itself: "the beautiful is always bizarre."[13]

This growing taste for free beauty, which Kant's text—accidentally, so to speak—has helped foster and privilege in Western aesthetics, has coincided, very broadly speaking, with the decline in the political fortunes of equity in its freedom from the laws. Rule-irrelevance, which under the aspect of an aesthetic phenomenon flourishes in Kant, has, as a prerogative of the head of state in the administering of justice, fallen out of favor, attacked by the antiabsolutist discourse of the rule of law and the independence of the judiciary. The approbation once accorded the "God-like Prince" in the justice of his suspension of the letter of the law is henceforth more comfortable with objects of free beauty, with the flowers, hummingbirds, musical fantasias, and the like to which we respond with a pleasure that, according to Kant, neither conformity to a general concept (the object pleases in its singularity) nor adequacy to an external end (the pleasure is disinterested) manages to explain.[14] The term "grace," in the polysemy with which it refers both to the mercy that commutes sentences and the elegance of manner that cannot be taught, attests to these negotiations over the respective extensions of the political and aesthetic domains. Viewed in this light, the aesthetic realm is as much a hideout as a holding cell for a political idea, a place in which the prerogative abused by despots is rendered innocuous or else bides its time, rallying its energies.[15]

In *The Scarlet Empress* the royal prerogative dissolves into the more pervasive rule-irrelevance of the characters of farce. The Tsarina Elizabeth, who is bound by no law, no more knows what she is doing than the various members of the imperial household. Louise Dresser, who had herself earlier played the part of Catherine the Great in the Rudolph Valentino vehicle *The Eagle* (1925), determinedly dispels any aura that might be thought to radiate from the person and office of the monarch. With her sporadic outbursts of peevish temper, her mangling of court procedure—at one point she solemnizes with an upraised turkey leg instead of the royal scepter—and her homespun Midwestern American accent, she is too small for her role and for that very reason also explodes it. There is to *The Scarlet Empress* something of a children's re-enactment of a witnessed but misunderstood parental drama: that the characters have to pile up in some numbers in order to budge the oversized doors with their handles at head height is only the most flagrant indication that a rescaling has occurred.

Dietrich's Catherine, who is the outsider at the Russian court, enters a setting where the challenge cannot be to find one's proper place, given that the very notion of the proper does not apply. The tyrannical unpredictability of the Empress Elizabeth is not the only issue at hand. Having been selected to marry the Grand Duke Peter (Sam Jaffe) and charged on arrival with the production of a male heir, Catherine discovers that her intended husband has no interest whatsoever in the match, abandoning her to her own devices while he plays with his toy soldiers with the Countess Elizabeth (Ruthelma Stevens). The elaborate, grandiose, and grotesque marriage ceremony does not serve to establish Catherine's position at court. For Sternberg, it is not a story worth the telling if the narrative trajectory that

FIGURE 3.1. The dinosaurs have died out and left us heirs to a world that is not to our scale: the ladies of the court struggle with a door in *The Scarlet Empress* (dir. Josef von Sternberg, Paramount Pictures, 1934).

Dietrich traces has her surrender her exceptionalism. If she stands out because of her beauty, if it is her beauty that cinematically gives the prerogative its substance, the comedy of *The Scarlet Empress* ensures that this aestheticization of the prerogative is at little risk of reversal—the loss of gravitas inflicted on the prerogative by aestheticization is compounded by the laughter that Dietrich by no means disdains to solicit.

In Dietrich's presentation of the film's title character, Catherine the Great is reimagined, so to speak, as Mae West, Dietrich's friend and neighbor on the Paramount lot. Dietrich's Catherine takes no time whatsoever to come of age. The Little Red Riding Hood of the first half of the film who greets all developments with a look of unshakable amazement gives way seemingly overnight to the worldly, sexually self-assured woman who signals a reassertion, indeed a magnification, of the familiar Dietrich persona. She does not so much bend to court ritual as invest it with the force of her own uninhibited desire. The formality of inspecting a line of soldiers in formation takes on a lewd literalness whose comic effect does not merely lie in the deviation from accepted custom. Dietrich's Catherine, openly flirting with the soldiers in front of her, runs her eyes admiringly over their bodies: as a genuine inspection of the guard, the scene pushes a case for being considered the humorously perverse truth of a traditional practice. *The Scarlet Empress*, disavowing any knowledge of the normal workings of power, explicates Catherine's political success in terms of her sexual generosity toward the palace regiment. The film thus carries a step further the logic according to which the "good looks" of a Hollywood star are the necessary point of entry for a republican audience's sympathetic engagement with the life story of a European aristocrat or crowned head of state. It is an extension that lays bare the political aggression latent in this approach to the casting of costume dramas. Here sex makes sense of power and sends up its pompousness and oppressiveness at the same time. Not content with the social contract's version of consent that Hobbes professes to discern even in despotism, the film explains Catherine's rise to dominance by means of a series of voluntary sexual liaisons: hers is the one government that can make good its claim to rest on consent (and not just, as in *Leviathan*, on the myth of consent articulated by an empirically unsubstantiated original covenant).

Catherine's apparently overnight transformation from an innocent abroad to "the ill-famed Messalina of the North" involves an elision of her pregnancy. Disillusioned with Count Alexei (John Lodge) on learning of his clandestine nocturnal meetings with the Tsarina Elizabeth, Catherine tramples the locket that he had given her containing his miniature and throws it out the window. The locket and its chain then proceed to slither downward from branch to branch in a floodlit courtyard with painted trees. When a breathless Catherine descends to retrieve it for reasons undisclosed, she is accosted by two soldiers, one of whom pulls her away in the direction of the guardhouse with a view to ascertaining her identity:

CATHERINE. I told you who I am.

NIGHTWATCHMAN. Oh, come now. Stop joking. If you're the grand duchess, then I'm the grand duke.

CATHERINE. I wish you were!

NIGHTWATCHMAN. If I were the grand duke and you were the grand duchess, I wouldn't let you prowl through the night like this, like a pretty little kitten.

CATHERINE *nonplussed but then gathering her thoughts.* Suppose I didn't want to tell you who I really am. What would happen?

NIGHTWATCHMAN. On a night like this, anything might happen . . . if I'm fortunate.

CATHERINE. Well, Lieutenant, you are fortunate, very . . . fortunate.

She kisses him, and she now holds briefly behind his back the locket that she had been hiding behind hers, before letting it again slip from her fingers.

The shot dissolves to a tolling bell, which in turn dissolves to a cannon discharging beneath a diorama of a Russian cityscape. This is followed by crowd scenes lifted from *The Patriot* (1928) by the reputedly more economical Lubitsch, who later as Paramount's production manager was to hold Sternberg's extravagance against him (this act of in-house piracy was welcome to Sternberg because it likewise enabled him to duck a location shoot). A baby boy has been born, yet instead of Catherine in her childbed it is Elizabeth who is seen lying beside the new male heir. She interrupts the ladies of the court who are fussing over him:

ELIZABETH *with increasing vehemence.* I don't want anyone near him unless I know about it, not even his mother. I had enough trouble getting him. If he catches cold or sniffles just once, I'll have you hung by the ears! If he coughs, I'll have you cut in half! And if anyone touches him, I'll have you shot!

Rewarding Catherine for having produced a male heir to the throne, Elizabeth sends her a jeweled necklace. In a half-slumber in a gigantic, luminous bed crowded over by statues, Catherine receives the gift and dangles it before her, in a visual echo of her earlier handling of Count Alexei's locket. And like the latter, it slips from her hand. The close-up is shot through the veil surrounding the bed, with the multifarious differences in textures between Dietrich's face, the ruffles and satin of her dress, the glinting jewel, and the sheets and pillowcase exploring the chromatic possibilities of whiteness. It would be a mistake to think that Sternberg here abandons himself to his enchantment with his star. A further dissolve to a tolling bell recalls the bell from the beginning of the film in which a suspended man was tortured: the pealing bells that celebrate the birth of a royal heir and, by extension, the consolidation of Catherine's position at court thus also herald the day when the young Sophia's daydreams of despotic license will be put into practice.

The irony with which Sternberg handles the voluptuousness of Dietrich's appearance in this scene has as much, if not more to do with the so-called battle of the sexes than with the sobering truth behind the façade of Tsarist Russia. Sternberg plays at believing that the two are interchangeable: by enlisting the latter as a symbol of the disillusionments and defeats of the former, he pretends and wishes that despotism as a political phenomenon no longer has any meaning in itself. The despotism into which *The Scarlet Empress* enquires is skin-deep. To see through Sternberg's Catherine is not to see her at all, not even as an autocrat in the making. Catherine, as Sternberg films her, is herself a Potemkin village. All is not as it seems, although there is nothing other than semblance. The semblance deceives without concealing anything: it leads astray in broad daylight. What deception there is, however, consists in self-deception, in mistaking one's pleasure in an appearance for the goodwill with which an appearance might be credited in the exercise of its power. In its commitment to its own illusionism, *The Scarlet Empress* is a cinema of the simulacrum. Russia does not stand up as its external referent.

In *Jet Pilot* (1957), the beleaguered Howard Hughes production on which Sternberg briefly worked from a screenplay by his former collaborator Jules Furthman, Russia similarly struggles to retain any reality in the maelstrom of appearances at whose center Sternberg places his female star. At least in an early scene whose wit and technical inventiveness suggest Sternberg's involvement (but whose breast-fixation is more characteristic of Russ Meyer), the Cold War is no more than a pretext for dwelling on the alleged dangers posed by Janet Leigh's physical charms. Taken into custody on an U.S. military airbase, Leigh's Lt. Anna Marladovna makes no attempt at a Russian accent and when informed that she will have to be searched, she removes layer after layer of her clothing in front of a comically discombobulated John Wayne to the expertly cued accompaniment of the roar of fighter planes passing overhead. If there is a battle of the sexes for Sternberg, he has scant interest in winning it. The world of his cinema, in its unrealistic effects and accentuations, is a phenomenologist's reconstruction of a woman's victory.

At the end of *The Scarlet Empress* Catherine herself pulls on the bell rope to announce the palace coup that sweeps her to power. The final words of the film are spoken by the guard before he disposes of the obstacle presented by her husband Peter, strangling him as he clutches a giant Suppedaneum cross: "There is no emperor, there is only an empress." Dressed in a white hussar's uniform and mounting a white horse, Catherine charges with her retinue down corridors, across courtyards, and up a staircase rattling with hooves to a musical mélange of the "Ride of the Valkyries," "Marche Slave," and the "1812 Overture," which Sternberg himself is said to have conducted. Catherine's apotheosis has her breathing heavily, her eyes blazing, her lips glistening, and her mouth wide open and grinning—she is the maenad to Garbo's shipboard Egyptian sphinx at the end of *Queen Christina*. Superimposed over Dietrich's face shot in a tight close-up is footage, taken from below, of her flag-bearing cavalrymen, itself superimposed on footage of the set's rendition of Orthodox icon painting.[16] It is a very different Catherine from the one who earlier, on the same staircase, shrank from Count Alexei's advances. When she protests that she will always remain faithful to her husband, he replies: "Those ideas are old-fashioned. This is the eighteenth century." Catherine, in asserting herself and in modernizing her attitudes to Count Alexei's liking, finds that it is the familiar cross-dressing Dietrich who has irrupted into Russian history.

This emergence of the star from behind the role does not, of course, in this instance amount to the intrusion of reality on a work of fiction (even if stars resemble the subjects of a documentary in avowing the presence of the camera).[17] Illusion as such is not shattered; instead, the artfully cultivated Dietrich persona lays claim to Catherine the Great as one further facet of its own artifice. Sophia Frederica's journey eastward from Prussia to the Russian court becomes a variation on Dietrich's journey westward from Berlin to Hollywood.[18] Catherine comes to herself, in Sternberg's burlesque redaction of the *Bildungsroman*, by drawing into alignment with Dietrich's image as star. Her self-knowledge dissolves what little historical concreteness the film was prepared to concede her. No less than the simultaneously rickety and overworked sets that were thrown up on a Paramount sound stage and immediately dismantled and recycled upon the completion of shooting, the anachronistic costumes and hairstyles hold at bay the perfection of an illusion of eighteenth-century court life. Catherine, whose passage from provincial naiveté to worldly self-possession is made to turn on the sexual liaisons she initiates, finds that her position has been usurped by the Dietrich myth. *The Scarlet Empress* does not merely replace the self-knowledge of the *Bildungsroman* with carnal knowledge, for in giving the Dietrich persona the upper hand over Catherine it denies the latter the conviction that she has come to herself in her series of sexual encounters with the soldiers of the palace regiment. To attribute to the Dietrich persona, as a transitory amalgam of studio lighting, musteline pelts, and glossy lipstick, the self-knowledge unavailable to Catherine is to insist on subjectivity where only its pure image is at stake.

The film's opening makes a gesture toward setting the "young" Sophia up for disillusionment. Descending a spiral staircase, Sophia bustles into the reception room where she bobs to kiss the hands of her assembled seated relatives: the Mickey Mousing from a string orchestra takes over the task of presenting the childishness for which Dietrich is unqualified, both temperamentally and physically. She asks Count Alexei, who has arrived to conduct her from her home to the Russian court, if he has brought a portrait of the man she has been chosen to marry (he had just given a miniature of the Empress Elizabeth to Sophia's father):

COUNT ALEXEI. I'm sorry, I did not. Would you like him to be handsome?

SOPHIA. Isn't he?

COUNT ALEXEI. Would you like him to be better looking than all other men, tall and gracious?

SOPHIA. Yes, I think I would.

COUNT ALEXEI. Well, he is all that and more. He's the handsomest man in the Russian court, tall, and formed like a Greek god, a model in fashion and deportment which all of us strive to follow. Are you eager to see him?

SOPHIA. Yes.

COUNT ALEXEI. His eyes are like the blue sky, his hair the colour of ebony. He is stronger than a team of oxen, and sleepless because of his desire to receive you in his arms. And he can also read and write.

This exchange concludes with a shot reverse shot that contrasts the ripely performed Count Alexei, talking through clenched teeth and devouring Sophia with his eyes, with a babyishly lisping, open-mouthed Dietrich.[19] When Count Alexei calls Sophia "a vision of loveliness," her mother glowers in a close-up that is as abrupt as the rap on the knuckles that she is not in a position to deliver.

Sternberg reprises this shot reverse shot of Count Alexei and Catherine at the latter's wedding ceremony. In an elaborately edited sequence Catherine at first glares balefully at Count Alexei, reproaching him for being the instrument of her deception regarding the new husband at her side, the idiotically grinning Grand Duke Peter. But as an awareness of the gravity of her predicament gains the upper hand over her indignation, her look changes to one of mute entreaty. In a procession of cuts Dietrich's face looms to monumental proportions, in an overcrowded set that is a fire hazard of religious iconography, dripping candles, veils, and fake eyelashes. Yet because it is the Empress Elizabeth who engineered the match and who literally oversees it, the camera ascends to her by means of a crane, with the scene closing on her face as it beams with self-satisfaction.

The wedding banquet that follows commences with a Mizoguchi-esque tracking shot plotting an irregular U-shaped course above the overladen table and surfeited guests. The first object it takes in, to the debauched and plaintive strains of a gypsy violin, is a human skeleton bent over a bubbling cauldron. It is a feast in a time of plague (or a booze-up in a robbers' den). With her diadem cockeyed, the Empress Elizabeth runs an unfocused gaze over the barbaric abundance of foodstuffs before her and the clumsy statuary strewn among it. The differential stylization in the attitudes and poses of the individual characters—no guest is allowed to resemble any other—invests the scene with a Meyerholdian air: arguably the influence that *The Scarlet Empress* was to exert on Eisenstein's *Ivan the Terrible: Part 1* (1944) and *Part 2* (1958) is, in some measure, through a confirmation of Eisenstein's preexisting commitment to Meyerhold's approach to blocking, gesture, and the handling of character. If the Empress Elizabeth is cheerful drunkenness and Catherine virginal shyness, then Count Alexei is resignation in defeat whereas Catherine's mother, daintily resorting to the finger bowl that a servant holds aloft beside her with a lady-in-waiting then to dry her hand, is the social climber's smugness. Sternberg continues his pan to the Countess Elizabeth who, slouching back in her chair with her shoulders up and tightened in defensiveness and her left hand curling under her chin, incarnates sullen resentment. The benevolent paternalism with which the Orthodox father (Davison Clark) comes then to rest his face on his right hand contrasts in its turn with the nervous twitching of Peter's retreat into fantasy. Sternberg returns to Catherine who scans her surroundings, lowers her head, and heaves a sigh. A guest picks up the head of a pig and bites off the snout. At the Empress Elizabeth's signal, the music stops, and Count Alexei raises a toast to Catherine, making no mention of her husband. The film flicks to another genre. After some comic business that would not be out of place in a pantomime, the Empress Elizabeth departs to the accompaniment of an extradiegetic brass band.

The bashfulness of Catherine's demeanor during the course of her wedding does not prove that she feels overwhelmed by her circumstances. It becomes a component in her "act," the weaponized coyness that she puts into service in her rise to power. To the extent that the Dietrich persona intrudes upon and informs the role of Catherine the latter's shyness fruitlessly labors to be read at face value. Encountering Alexei in the stables, Catherine says nothing to encourage him in his pursuit of her. But holding on to a rope at head height and with her face assuming the blankness of a doll's, she rocks from side to side and then falls backward into the hay where Alexei hurries to join her. No sooner has he plucked one ear of wheat from her mouth than she coquettishly replaces it:

CATHERINE. If you come closer, I'll scream.
COUNT ALEXEI. It will be easier for you to scream without a straw in your mouth.

Yet once there is nothing between her lips, she kisses Alexei instead. In terms of Catherine's narrative, an innocent is here being seduced. But in terms of the Dietrich persona, there is no innocence to lose and certainly none to mourn.

For it to be clear that it is the Dietrich persona that comes to power at the end of the film, Catherine must keep her distance from the machinations of the court. As her victory is to be a matter of her appearance alone, she rebuffs an offer of ecclesiastical assistance:

CATHERINE. How could *you* be of help?

FATHER. I control enough of the political machine to carry some weight in a crisis.

CATHERINE *smiling*. I have no wish to share in any petty conspiracy. Should it become unavoidable, I think I have weapons (*playfully raising and lowering a veil over her mouth*) that are far more powerful than any political machine.

FATHER. I'm afraid you don't know Russians, my child.

CATHERINE. That's possible, father, but I'm taking lessons as fast as I can.

Catherine's position at court is precarious once the Empress Elizabeth's health declines, although the more Catherine disappears into Dietrich's appearance, the less she credits the dangers that lie in wait for her. The prospect of his aunt's demise, having emboldened Peter to smuggle the Countess Elizabeth back from the exile to which the Empress had banished her, prompts him to envisage not only replacing his wife, but furthermore doing away with her altogether: he chops off the head of a doll and asks Catherine what she thinks of this "de-Cathitation." If Catherine feels at risk, Dietrich has no grounds to participate in the sentiment, floating as she is in this scene on a sea of white ostrich feathers while immured in the invulnerability of mere appearance:

CATHERINE. How is Astrakhan, Lizzie? Or was it Afghanistan?

COUNTESS ELIZABETH. If you're wise, you'll find out for yourself before it's too late! There are some very comfortable convents along the way, and all you have to do to gain admission is shave your head. It's good for the scalp, anyway!

CATHERINE. Entirely too many men love my hair, and I have no intention of changing my residence.

Catherine-as-Dietrich—for it is not Dietrich playing the role of Catherine, but rather the historical figure of Catherine who has turned herself into the Dietrich persona—has grasped that the world over which she is to rule does not extend beyond the borders of the shot. The resources on which she can rely are limited to what is visible at any given moment. She is the tyrant who understands that her domain is cinema. As such, she is the image of autonomy but no more than its image. It is only as an image that the history of despotism can be redeemed because it is only as an image, in its flatness and phantasmality, that this history bears remembering (misremembering). The rule-irrelevance of the beautiful image that *The Scarlet Empress* substitutes for the license of the despot is in its own way as much of a condemnation of European autocracy as the farce in which it features.

While carnival lasts, there is no other life outside it.
MIKHAIL BAKHTIN

4 *The Devil Is a Woman*
AGAINST THE OFF-SCREEN

THE DEVIL IS *a Woman* (1935), Sternberg's final collaboration with Dietrich, is a complex and superficial film. It is composed of vignettes and tableaux showcasing its star that purposely do not add up to a whole. The framing story in which Don Pasqual (Lionel Atwill) relates to Antonio (Cesar Romero) the dolorous history of his liaison with Concha Perez (Dietrich) does not coordinate the successive images, providing them with the articulation that they themselves disdain. Individual shots and sequences bristle with a kind of feral independence in which the immediacy of the visual attempts to banish all other considerations. Don Pasqual's framing story, because he proves himself to be an undependable narrator, does not stand in for the world. It does not fit the cinematic cells together and re-establish the coherence of the world; indeed, it stands guard over their disjointedness, impeding readings of the film that would approach its shots and scenes as jigsaw pieces abstracted from the one totality. Refusing to be hammered into place within a whole, the images of *The Devil Is a Woman* problematize the notion of the off-screen, for they defy the services of unseen space in puttying shots into larger representative units that both encompass and transcend the visual. There is thus a candid idolatry to *The Devil Is a Woman* in its absolutism of the visual: what you see is what you get.[1]

A cinema that adopts an antagonistic attitude toward the off-screen is a cinema that wants to rethink its relationship to truth. Wherever the image oscillates in the invisible presence of the off-screen, wherever this invisibility is held to be inexhaustible, there is a world that looms up as the transcendental horizon of proceedings and the site of an image's truth or falsehood. This world is not a fact of the film, but rather a practice of the viewer by means of which images are interpreted as clues that call out for a world to contain them and to make sense of them. Inasmuch as it attests to something beyond its frame, the image is a fragment and its edges do not so much close it off as open it out. An image can lie about this larger world, and it can also contribute to the fabrication of a world of lies. The correlation of images undertaken by the off-screen allows for a given image to be shown up as mendacious or confirmed as true with respect to the putative world of the film. The world of a film can be the internal interconnection and plausibility of its fictional narrative or the deceptive construct that its makers substitute for the world at large, just as it also can be identified by the observable facts of a previously experienced extracinematic reality. An individual image can be grasped as lying about the world of the film in which it appears so long as this world and its other images are held to rally in contestation of it. For all their disregard of the truth, the makers of propaganda are rarely satisfied with the creation of images alone: they want their images to call into being a larger world in which they will count as true. What differentiates Sternberg's film from propaganda is that its spectacle does not pretend to represent a world that transcends it. It does not enlist the off-screen in order to press a claim to truth.

How does Sternberg prevent a world from congealing around his images?[2] The multiple prongs of his strategy can be brought out by an analysis of the unresolved nature of the narrative, the inconsistencies of Dietrich's character, and the claustrophobically self-contained composition of many of the shots. The screenplay by John Dos Passos, adapted from *La Femme et le Pantin* (1898) by Pierre Louÿs, incorporates a suite of scenes illustrating the romantic recollections that Don Pasqual shares with Antonio. But the film does not set Don Pasqual up as a trustworthy narrator. He has more than one motive for not depicting Concha to Antonio as she is: by maligning her to Antonio he might hope to persuade a rival to "leave the field" just as his extreme ambivalence toward her does not mark him out as a dispassionate witness. And yet in suspecting the veracity of the portrait of Concha that emerges in the visual rendition of Don Pasqual's tale, the audience cannot expect to light upon an image of the true Concha in the scenes before and after Don Pasqual's illustrated conversation with Antonio. If the lie of Don Pasqual's Concha does not shatter on contact with the truth of Concha as she is in the world outside a lover's jealous misrepresentations, it is because there is no world in which she is more than an image.[3]

The reason for this, as Carole Zucker argues, is that the notable inscrutability of Dietrich's character in her earlier films with Sternberg is now a polished façade without any chink whatsoever:

> If in viewing Dietrich's previous incarnations we harboured notions of interpreting her "acts" and thus understanding something about her character, in *The Devil Is a Woman* this knowledge is blocked. In Dietrich's final film with Sternberg she seems to offer herself, posing as a seductress, then rescinding her proposition. Dietrich *shows* us an attitude, but does not *tell* why it is either offered *or* withdrawn; she performs actions that do not reveal anything beyond themselves. In the earlier films we are drawn into a labyrinth that provides a multitude of paths leading to Dietrich's roles, Dietrich and Sternberg. In *The Devil Is a Woman* the maze presents a series of dead ends, obstructions that are impassable, questions that neither the performance nor the director claim to answer.[4]

Dietrich's Concha is a succession of looks, poses, and actions that do not converge in the suggestion of a character with a life and substance beyond the frame. The truth of who she is cannot be discovered through any astute reassembly of the shards and splinters of her cinematic self.

Concha is unpredictable because prediction entails extrapolating from a given image to a future agency. Although Don Pasqual portrays Concha as a femme fatale to Antonio, she does not conform to that image once his framing story is done with. Her fickleness is not the unreliability for which the notion of the femme fatale supplies a psychological explanation. The concluding scene does not corroborate Don Pasqual's fears of Concha's heartlessness. She does not run off with Antonio with whom Don Pasqual had fought a duel for her sake and whose life he spared. But even if it is clear that Concha has not followed through on her plan to accompany Antonio to Paris, her statement at the border that she is going back to Don Pasqual invites being taken, as Charles Silver notes, with a grain of salt:

> All that we know of Concha until the end of the film was conveyed through the eyes and the mouths of the men. Perhaps these were all lies, and now we are seeing her for the first time as she really is. And since we never see Dietrich reunited with Atwill, we don't even know whether she was telling Romero the truth.[5]

The steam of the departing train's engine envelops Antonio's anguished and bewildered face and Concha settles down to smoke a cigarette offered her by a coachman.[6]

As Zucker contends, *The Devil Is a Woman* is the apogee of the direction on which Dietrich embarked in her very first film with Sternberg. One of the methods that Dietrich regularly employs to seal the shot in which she appears, thereby warding off communication with the off-screen, is her refusal to maintain eye contact with her interlocutors. By glancing back and forth to the upper right and to the upper left, she frustrates the eyeline matches whereby the various individual shots of a scene can be read as appertaining to the one space. What, theatrically speaking, is rather rudimentary code for embodying a character whose mind is on something other than what is under discussion becomes, in Dietrich's hands and with Sternberg's collusion, a means for working against the subordination of cinema to the precept of the unity of space.

The shot variations by which D. W. Griffith, among other early pioneers, radically enhanced film's storytelling capacity always nurtured this other possibility of deploying montage against the very idea of a world. No matter how violent and nihilistic the commercial cinema of action may be in the content of its images, it must be deemed restorationist when its editing practices are measured against Sternberg's. Confronted with shots that differ in the scaling of objects, in the choice of angle and lens, a viewer can be prompted to sublate these differences in a spatial continuum. An action and its consequences form the red thread that links up the individual shots and recovers the prima facie heterogeneity of their spaces for a single world. The commercial cinema's commitment to the world-conjuring powers of action is, more precisely, a commitment to action's consequences, for it is in rippling out beyond the edges of the frame in which the action is shot that consequences evoke a world larger than the individual image. From this vantage point, the commercial cinema of action does not so much display a naïve faith in human agency as a resignation of the work of montage to the natural laws of cause and effect. The continuity of action cinema differs in kind from the continuity furnished by the persistence of one or more given characters in succeeding scenes insofar as the character is interpreted as a discrete visual mass within the shot. In piecing together the various shots in which it and its effects are shown, an action constitutes the overlap that informs the status of attention accorded to whatever in the shot is not repeated. This is not at all to imply that the singularities of a given shot are routinely ignored, but it is to submit that an action-focused mode of viewing a film quickly arrives at a set of weightings by which it evaluates the singularities of any succeeding image: that which does not illuminate or further the action is consigned to the background.

The decadence with which Sternberg luxuriates in the visuals of a scene flouts the hierarchized perception that a viewer drilled in the continuity of the commercial cinema of action brings to bear. Dietrich's dizzying changes of costume conspire to unhinge the world that might otherwise consolidate in the viewer's head. The images of *The Devil Is a Woman*, being images pure and simple, are not representations of a world: they do not summon up a world that extends beyond the borders of the image within which a portion of it is captured and that, being common to every shot, reconciles them.[7]

Following André Bazin, a cinema that repudiates the off-screen attenuates its difference from both painting and theater:

> Because it is only part of the architecture of the stage, the decor of the theater is thus an area materially enclosed, limited, circumscribed. [. . .] It exists by virtue of its reverse side and its absence from anything beyond, as the painting exists by virtue of its frame. Just as the picture is not to be confounded with the scene it represents and is not a window in a wall. The stage and the decor where the action unfolds constitute an aesthetic microcosm inserted perforce into the universe but essentially distinct from the Nature which surrounds it. It is not the same with cinema, the basic principle of which is a denial of any frontiers to action. [. . .] When a character moves off screen, we accept the fact that he is out of sight, but he continues to exist in his own capacity at some other place in the decor which is hidden from us. There are no wings to the screen.[8]

According to Bazin's exposition, the off-screen is an essential component of the act of viewing a film. It is less an actuality of the physical artifact that is film than a cognitive supplement in the viewer's perceptual process: it resembles the blank space in a sliding puzzle without which the game cannot be played. And because it is not a part of the film itself as physical artifact, a filmmaker cannot simply decide to dispense with it. The campaign against the off-screen has to be conducted within the viewer's head. If a film such as *The Devil Is a Woman* does not collapse into being a theatrical performance or a painting, it is because it can never take its victory over the off-screen as given in advance of the act of perception. It has to apply its energies to aborting the birth of a world in the viewer's head, whereas a theatrical performance or painting need not concern itself with this eventuality.

The stubbornness with which viewers attribute cosmogenesis to cinema can be discerned in Noël Burch's inventively obtuse account of the dressing rooms in *The Blue Angel*. The space in which Lola Lola and Professor Immanuel Rath first meet opens out in so many different directions that it ceases, as Burch all but acknowledges, to be an intelligible world:

> The crucial strategy here is the use of a pair of doors constantly opening and closing in a marvelously complicated pattern; snatches of music, bursts of applause, and scraps of dialogue drift in as the doors are open and are cut off as they shut, each time in a different relation to the editing scheme. A structure

of variations results that is exemplary in its rigor. Sometimes one of the doors (which one?—they all look alike and the space these dressing rooms define is one of the most totally abstract in cinema, analyzable only in terms of what each successive "composition" reveals) opens off screen, there is a sudden burst of music, followed by a shot of the door, which is then closed again. Sometimes a door opens on screen, the shot then shows something else, and it closes off screen. At times, the door opens or closes at the junction of two shots; at times, the door is opened or closed without affecting the ambient sounds—another unseen door perhaps has remained open.[9]

Otto Hunte's sets for *The Blue Angel* do not defer to the logic and conventions of theatrical architecture. Lola Lola, as the principal attraction of the company, has a two-storeyed dressing room that is nonetheless also something of a thoroughfare through which all and sundry, including a dancing bear, feel at liberty to pass. The abstractness that Burch ascribes to this space can have nothing to do with a lack of embellishments (every surface betrays Sternberg's preference for clutter) but corresponds instead to its aggression toward the known world from which it seeks to twist itself loose.

FIGURE 4.1. Emil Jannings as Immanuel Rath puffs himself up when Kurt Gerron as Kiepert discovers him in the makeshift dressing room that Marlene Dietrich occupies as Lola Lola in *The Blue Angel* (dir. Josef von Sternberg, UFA, 1930).

When a door shuts in this scene, the sound coming supposedly from outside the dressing room does not continue in a muffled form, but abruptly breaks off (this is not the level of soundproofing one would expect from a turn-of-the-century beer hall). To put down the unnaturalness of the effect to Sternberg and his crew's inexperience in the making of a sound film is to discount the artistic ambition with which they approached this new dimension of the cinematic image. The sounds that irrupt with the opening of a door testify to a space beyond the dressing rooms. Yet in the brusqueness with which they begin and end, they pointedly declare themselves to be the mediated and reproduced testimony of such a soundscape rather than the phenomenon itself. The soundtrack has swallowed the off-screen and exploits it for artistic effects. Emancipated from realism, off-screen sounds become available for use as interjections and interruptions that compound the awkwardnesses of Lola Lola and Rath's first meeting. This space in which Rath makes the acquaintance of the woman he is to marry is allowed neither visually nor aurally to curl up into a lovers' retreat: the outside world exists solely as an *on-screen* disturbance of the cinematic correlate that another filmmaker might be tempted to contrive for a folie à deux.

Sternberg's chariness in the face of the "natural" relationship that seeks to install itself between the image and the off-screen has a basis in his care for the efficacy and freshness of the image. The off-screen, in its office of pulling the image out beyond itself, is instrumental in binding one image to another in a world that is common but not reducible to them. To beat down the demands for the off-screen is to let the image press the case for its self-referentiality. Compared with a hypothetical film in which each shot is taken up entirely by the canvas of a different painting, *The Devil Is a Woman*, needless to say, does not go so far in prizing its component images loose of any relation to an off-screen. But then Sternberg does not want to jump over the photographic image so much as to endue it with unexpected values (to use Sternberg's own term). The photographic image, where it does not restrict itself to the technological reproduction of a painting, inexorably brings with it associations with the off-screen inasmuch as the act of framing involves the exclusion of a determinate, perceptible profilmic reality to the left and right, above and below the camera.[10] The off-screen as a memory of the technological process of filming carries over, however illegitimately, to the off-screen as the spatial glue of the various shots of a cinematic fiction (the unseen space of the studio in which a film is produced scarcely ever agrees with the unseen space that in the viewer's head combines with the shots to make up the world of the narrative).

By trying to counteract the entrenchment of the narrative off-screen in *The Devil Is a Woman*, Sternberg cautions the viewer of Don Pasqual's illustrated tale against the non sequitur of inferring a reality apart from the images. Don Pasqual depicts

Concha to Antonio as a woman who cannot be trusted. Inasmuch as the variations in her attitudes and conduct can no more be reconciled than the variations in her wardrobe, there must necessarily exist a hidden—off-screen—self that oversees the variations and that is too morally corrupt to venture into the light of day. Yet Don Pasqual's stock diatribe against the duplicity of women is undercut by the revelation of the duplicity of Don Pasqual's own storytelling. The cinematic image, with its technological reproduction of the profilmic, turns out not to have been a passive recording of what is the case. In this respect, *The Devil Is a Woman* anticipates Hitchcock's *Stage Fright* (1950) in which Dietrich's character is first shown confessing to the murder of her husband, a confession that is subsequently designated a lie. In the case of *The Devil Is a Woman*, however, what was initially presented as true—namely, Don Pasqual's version of his past dealings with Concha—is not then reclassified as false so much as unreliable. This unreliability sets an image free from its world, for the ascertainable truth or falsehood of an image is a matter of its relation to a world. Unlike the negative reception of *Stage Fright*, which focused on the lying flashback that Hitchcock later regretted including, the negative reception of *The Devil Is a Woman* was embarrassed, so to speak, by the wealth of its grievances against the film.

As Sternberg recalls it in his autobiography, the projected and more fitting name for this image-obsessed film, *Capriccio Espagnol*, was vetoed by Lubitsch and replaced with *The Devil Is a Woman*: "This accent is not mine. Though Mr. Lubitsch's poetic intention to suggest altering the sex of the devil was meant to aid in selling the picture, it did not do so."[11] Orphaned passages from Rimsky-Korsakov's *Capriccio Espagnol* (1887) remain on the soundtrack, most notably during the opening credits. Sternberg's and Lubitsch's respective misogynies were not in step. The well-known, early distribution woes of *The Devil Is a Woman* can be traced back to a willful discounting of the image's resistance to the business of reference. A documentary is not at stake: Sternberg aspires less to an image of Spain than to a free handling of Spanish imagery—a cinematic counterpart to the treatment of folk melodies in Rimsky-Korsakov's orchestral suite. Dietrich's Concha fends off the reality of Spain as much as she gestures toward it. There is thus a note of bemused irritation in Sternberg's reminiscences three decades after the work's release:

> The film was banned by the Spanish government, which, in turn, was banned by Generalissimo Franco, but not before its diplomats made protestations to our government that caused the work to be withdrawn from circulation. The ostensible reason given was that the Guardia Civil had been shown to be ineffectual in curbing a riotous carnival during which the action of the film takes place.[12]

The freedom that Sternberg had sought to invest in the image was taken for carica-ture and misrepresentation, and the resulting financial loss incurred by Paramount from *The Devil Is a Woman* led to the termination of Sternberg's relationship with the studio. He was never again to have at his command the resources that Paramount had placed at his disposal. His subsequent commissions for Columbia and RKO in-volved multiple compromises and concessions, and when he recovered his earlier degree of directorial control, in the making of *The Saga of Anatahan* (1953), it was under severe budgetary constraints. If in comparison with *The Scarlet Empress, The Devil Is a Woman* is not obviously polemical, the Spanish government, unlike that of the Soviet Union, was in a position to win a hearing for its complaints in Washington (whereas Sternberg's career faltered in the wake of the Spanish government's indig-nation over *The Devil Is a Woman*, John Lodge, who had played Count Alexei in *The Scarlet Empress*, went on by a curious twist of fate to serve as U.S. Ambassador in Madrid).

In his chronicle of the woes that beset both the shooting and the afterlife of the film, Sternberg recounts the making of Dietrich's opening scene:

> The few who have seen this film might recall how my Concha, for so Marlene was named in the film, first appears in the turmoil of the carnival. Her face concealed by swaying toy balloons, she stands in a horse-drawn carriage, making its way through a masked and boisterous crowd of revellers. The scene shows a sling used by one of the masked men who wishes to attract her atten-tion. [. . .] Neither of us would have permitted anyone else to shoot a pellet from a rifle at the wavering target of her covered face. When the scene began, I took aim and exploded the concealing balloons to reveal one of the most fearless and charming countenances in the history of films. Not a quiver of an eyelash, nor the slightest twitch in the wide gleaming smile was recorded by the camera at a time when anyone other than this extraordinary woman would have trembled in fear.[13]

The passage, in which Sternberg admits to terrorizing his star during the course of shooting, ends with a compliment to Dietrich's imperturbability in the presence of danger. The artistic rationale for Sternberg's behavior—if indeed there is any—does not line up with any diegetic revelation of her character's composure behind a burst balloon, for what he describes belongs to the prehistory of the close-up contained in the finished film. The first sight of Dietrich's face does not follow on from the pop-ping of a balloon in the film; instead, she appears in a *plan américain*, framed rather than concealed by balloons. What blocks her from view, albeit but fleetingly, are carriages traveling in the opposite direction. The subsequent close-up of Dietrich's "wide gleaming smile" is part of a shot reverse shot in which Antonio, the masked man who endeavors to attract Concha's attention by means of the judicious use of a sling, appears to catch her eye.[14] Yet without a dogmatic faith in the cinematic convention of eyeline matches, Dietrich's perennially roaming eye cannot be said to lend itself here to an aligning of her close-up with Antonio's. Where exactly Antonio stands in relation to Concha is not established by any shot that contains either the two of them or even objects or persons that have been in their vicinity and that could thus serve to orient the viewer in a common space. Balloons are heard bursting on the soundtrack, but they are not seen. As Concha's close-up did not call for a firearm to be aimed in Dietrich's direction, Sternberg's memoirs fraudulently attempt an aesthetic recuperation of his aggression toward her.

Yet putting to one side whatever psychological motivations might be attributed to Sternberg for this reimagining of the scene in an apologetics without an apology, one can also read the passage for its ex post facto distillation of his directorial attitude with respect to the ontological status of the image. On Sternberg's retelling, Dietrich makes her entrance by coming to the surface of the image rather than by breaching the frame. The misremembered scene is emblematic of Sternberg's management of off-screen space in this film in which the image asserts its self-sufficiency, asserts itself as an image of self-sufficiency. It is the key that was not issued with the work itself.

Dietrich emerges in *The Devil Is a Woman* as a creature of carnival. The demarcated sites of the entertainment industry that she inhabits in earlier films give way to a spectacle without onlookers. Carnival takes over public places and empties the private realm into it. The light of publicity illuminates without passing sentence: the image is evidence of nothing beyond its appearance. The carnival setting of *The Devil Is a Woman* allows Sternberg to continue his exploration of the floating life of images. Given that the content of the image is not his sole preoccupation, it would be a mistake to view the film as no more than an inventory of Iberian kitsch. All the trappings and appurtenances, stereotypes, and tics that Mérimée, Manet, Bizet, and other French artists already churned over in the nineteenth century concern a Spain that has become unmoored from reality. These images, in their own condition, replicate that suspension of the everyday which characterizes carnival. Carnival not only provides an abundance of imagery, but it furthermore sets up the image as simply an image. By virtue of its resistance to the passage of historical time, it retains folk practices that have otherwise disappeared, giving them a new lease on life as pure images, shorn of whatever functionality they once possessed.[15] As a kind of geological cross section in which different cultural formations are preserved, carnival can pass for a parade of superannuated clichés in the representation of a people. It is the pocket of regionalisms that has withstood in broad daylight the diffusion of a generic transnational modernity. For Dietrich to wear a mantilla and *peineta*, besides inviting charges of a heavy-handed and condescending cultural appropriation, is as much about the implausibility and irreality of the image as it is about referencing a recognizable Spain. Introduced as a deceiver, Dietrich's Concha lends credibility to Don Pasqual's account of her through her dubious impersonation of a lower-class Spanish woman. Given that it is not the business of a star to immerse herself in a role, Dietrich's performance involves the gravitational pull that her star persona exercises on the character assigned her in the film: Concha is lifted out of the environment that would otherwise enclose her just as Dietrich's image is itself plucked and tweaked in new directions.

The Concha that Antonio encounters during carnival is very different from the Concha of Don Pasqual's first meeting with her. When Antonio runs into Don Pasqual and asks him if he knows anything about Concha Perez, Don Pasqual invokes a cinematic reverie of the crowded train in which Dietrich sits in what verges on a nun's habit. It is one of Sternberg's most visually arresting compositions, exemplary in its distribution of light and shade. Although Concha wears a wimple and a crucifix necklace, the kiss curl and the stripes on her sleeves indicate that, notwithstanding the beatific radiance that singles her out among her fellow passengers, she has not altogether signed up for the simulation of the religious life. When Don Pasqual begins his account, his face dissolves to the accompaniment of high-pitched tremolo violin harmonics that, for their part, give way to the sound of a train whistle. The soundtrack changes again with the appearance of Dietrich inside the railway carriage. An impromptu flamenco recital has sprung up in the cramped quarters. Much to Concha's annoyance, a woman, jumping enthusiastically to her feet in order to dance, bumps with her shoulder the large wicker cage that hangs just to the left of Concha's head. Concha endeavors to steady the cage and priggishly swabs down her arm with a cloth, but the admonition imparted by the latter action is nonetheless lost on her ever-swirling assailant. Sticking out a foot, Concha then trips the woman, who hurtles against the wall and, turning with her hands on her hips, fixes Concha with an irate stare. Playing innocent, Concha bats her enormous eyelashes and twiddles her thumbs, but rather than rising to the bait of this additional provocation, the woman simply smiles and resumes her baile, conscious that her pleasure in her dancing is shared by everyone in the carriage apart from Concha. Even though there is also a smile on Concha's face, its inspiration lies elsewhere. When Concha trips the woman a second time, the music stops, and a brawl erupts. The woman splays the fingers of her hands and charges at Concha, who adopting in turn the part of a matador, performs a *suerte de capote* with the cloth with which she had mopped up the liquid that had trickled down on her sleeve. This is Don Pasqual's cue for his entrance.

FIGURE 4.2. Saintliness will turn out not to be responsible for the halo with which Marlene Dietrich is endowed as Concha Perez in *The Devil Is a Woman* (dir. Josef von Sternberg, Paramount Pictures, 1935).

That the scene arrives at a brawl is the joke for which the opening shot is the set-up. Concha's nun-like dress has no explanation outside the scene's own comic dynamics. The scene charts the unraveling of its opening shot whose pictorial perfection is surrendered to the impiety of the moving image. The joke is not merely that a nun, contrary to expectations, winds up instigating a riot. (The cheap surprise of such a gag is diluted in advance by the profane baggage of the Dietrich persona.) Don Pasqual's voice-over introduces the shot as the product of an avalanche that has impeded for three days the onward progress of the train. Dietrich borrows from the outward form of a nun just enough to differentiate her from all the other travelers. The diagonal lines of Concha's black veil repeat the angles of the top of the wicker cage, which in being jostled upsets the isomorphism of the composition. The ostensible tranquility of the religious life that Dietrich claims as her own in the opening shot is the tranquility of the stillness in which her neighbor does not permit her to remain. If, to begin with, there is in this shot something akin to a tableau vivant of Honoré Daumier's *The Third-Class Carriage* (1862–64), the requisite stasis quickly becomes ever more elusive. With her hood and the basket in her lap, Dietrich's Concha is diverted from any planned resemblance to the elderly woman at the center-left of Daumier's painting, for the moving image insists on what is proper to it. Yielding to its temptation to generate an illusion of depth, it alters the position of the planes of the various bodies in the shot. The woman who is at first seated behind Concha to her right is next standing in front of her and then dances off to her left. The belief in object permanence—the belief, specifically, that it is one and the same woman even as her size and position changes while she weaves her way among the obstacles in the shot—colludes with the maneuvers among the pictorial components to cast doubt on the two-dimensionality of the image, because the woman's movement is intelligible only on the assumption that there is space between the planes in view (for instance, between Concha and the back of the headstock of the guitar). The result of the ensuing mayhem is that Don Pasqual holds Concha back from the fray whereas Concha, who had let go of the goose with which she was traveling in order to free her hands for the mêlée, finds herself in possession not only of her original goose, but also of a human goose in the shape of Don Pasqual.[16]

Don Pasqual's hermeneutic misstep is that he looks for something other than the workings out of the internal dynamics of a shot. He makes a fool of himself by searching for motives that would coordinate Concha's various actions. For Barbara Bowman, the obscurity attending her characters' motives invests Dietrich's face with the mystery and intrigue of the off-screen.[17] One might add to this that Dietrich's face carries out in Sternberg's films some of the functions otherwise performed by the off-screen: it is a face that, by relieving him of the need for the off-screen and its dramatic prompts, facilitates a holism of the cinematic image. The visible takes on some of the properties of the invisible.

This demotion of the off-screen in *The Devil Is a Woman* corresponds to an idiosyncratic attitude toward the frame. As a technological fact that testifies to cinema's relationship to the profilmic, the frame almost seems to nettle Sternberg. He doubles it with multiple frames internal to the image as though he wanted to ward it off and to crowd it out. Streamers, vegetation, silhouettes cluster along the border of the shot, focusing the gaze as well as interposing their artifice between the illuminated center of the image and the brute mechanical given of the cinematic shot's rectilinear edges.

By playing down the constants of the straight lines of the cinematic frame, Sternberg distances himself from Bazin's vision of cinema as "a window onto the world."[18] Like the edges of the eye's visual field, Sternberg's borders are a zone of indeterminacy and indistinctness. His images, in their discomfort with the rigid horizontals and verticals of the cinematic frame, could thus be said to aspire to a perceptual realism. This realism of Sternberg's is not an affair of the world, given that it concerns the visible rather than the world off-screen that the crisp edge of the cinematic frame conjures up. If Bazin's realism has, in this regard, more in common with transcendental idealism than with positivism, it is because the world that a viewer is induced to intercalate between shots is not given to the senses. Sternberg's realism is a realism of the immanence of the image.

Whenever he manages to obstruct the world in the viewer's head that would otherwise envelop the images of *The Devil Is a Woman*, Sternberg strengthens the spectacle of the film. The image is not a prop in Kendall Walton's sense: it does not authorize the collective games of make-believe in which the appreciators of a work of art join in bearing witness to a fictional world.[19] Inasmuch as it does not lend itself to being used to look beyond it to a world, the image can only be looked at. In the absence of the truth that comes with a world, *The Devil Is a Woman* is nevertheless not cognitively vacuous when compared with other cinematic fictions: the spectacularism of the work cannot be translated into a general commitment to skepticism because what is being spurned is simply the truth of a fictional world rather than truth as such. A fiction that takes for granted its collaboration with the nongiven world that coordinates its parts risks trivializing the epistemic operation of the world: its microcosm is an image of the world put to sleep. By contrast, a spectacle to the extent that it is not brainless and involves the testing and rejection of interpretive hypotheses can be said to delay the consolidation not so much of the world itself, as of the habits, assumptions, prejudices, and conventions that pass for a world.

In "The Origin of the Work of Art" (1935–36), Heidegger writes: "To be a work means: to set up a world."[20] The work that does not set up a world is not a great work of art rather than not a work of art at all (Heidegger clarifies a little earlier in the text that his account applies only to great art).[21] Does it follow that *The Devil Is a Woman*, by virtue of its handling of off-screen space, cannot count as great art from Heidegger's perspective? The question, in one respect, is already answered in Heidegger's repudiation of cinema as a whole.[22] But even if his sweeping criticisms of cinema are disregarded, the position articulated in "The Origin of the Work of Art" does not justify a more favorable assessment of films whose relationship with off-screen space is less vexed than that of *The Devil Is a Woman,* because setting up a world differs from activating a predisposition to worlds in a viewer's mind. The world that the work of art sets up for Heidegger is the space that is larger than any use and that cannot be reduced to the intelligibility and coherence of phenomena. It enables the use and sense of the objects it encompasses just as it is, by extension, the condition of possibility of the off-screen space by means of which a viewer construes the discrete images of a film. In resisting the spell of off-screen space, *The Devil Is a Woman* calls attention to the somnolence of the modern world.[23] Unmoored from off-screen space, it could be taken to herald the messianic coming of a new world. But if it does so, it is not without ambiguity and qualification, without a bet each way on the desirability of this coming.

The world-weariness of the Dietrich persona is often belied in *The Devil Is a Woman*. There is an extravagant and infectious joy to her performance of Ralph Rainger and Leo Robin's song for chorus and principal, "Three Sweethearts Have I," and in her comically preposterous teasing of Don Pasqual she never becomes mired in his gravity. She does not move within the world. Images are her element and the more recognizable they are as images rather than as reality, the better. When Don Pasqual chances upon Concha again after the train trip on which they first met, it is in a cigarette factory pilfered shamelessly from *Carmen*. They leave alone together and although there is no reason to think that the scene takes place during carnival, the soundtrack is given over to a riotous crowd of women. The noise of carnival protects Concha from the everyday world.

Conclusion

TOWARD AN ETHICS OF THE MOVING IMAGE

CINEMA MAKES AN art out of looking. The framing of shots, the determining of the look of a scene becomes the pre-eminent site of artistic agency if only because so much of the actual formation of images is consigned to the technological automatism of the camera. After the initial and far-reaching intervention effected by the development of the camera, the agency of any individual filmmaker—if it is to find a place for itself at all—has to negotiate the passivity with which the apparatus records the profilmic. There is a difference in kind between the filmmaker and the painter, for although the representations that a painter can pull off are constrained by the expressive potentials of a given pigment, the undeployed pigment represents only itself. The image, by contrast, that concerns a filmmaker is, in a very palpable sense, already fully there before the camera starts rolling: the art is to see it.

The ethics of the cinematic image is accordingly not identical with the ethics of the older visual arts such as painting and sculpture. The filmmaker handles likenesses that are given to him or her profilmically rather than producing images that may be received in several ways depending on the intention and ability of the artist (as faithful portraits, idealizations, or defamatory caricatures). In other words, the intention and ability of the filmmaker apply to how the likeness is seen and not to how it first comes into being. The initial and abiding artifice of cinema, as a human invention, is complemented (or counteracted) by the factuality with which the profilmic stands before the camera. It is the lot of the profilmic in the age of cinema to be always ready to generate likenesses of itself. This is what renders the birth of cinema an event in the world history of simulacra, for it ushered into nature a new wave of likenesses, augmenting the crowd of shadows and reflections that already accompanied material beings.

It is of course true that painting and sculpture also occupy themselves with the look of their subjects, with the angle at which they are presented, and with the space by which they are framed. These are separate tasks even if they can be carried out at the same time as the likeness is produced. The look of the work of visual art, however, can only ever play at an independence from its subject, because what is looked at is also produced. This is not to deny a gap between the work's external referent and the latter's likeness in the work (the gap authorizes claims of accuracy or slander relating to the depiction), yet it is to deny that the image—and not just the raw materials such as paint and marble from which the artist composes it—can be reasonably credited with an independence from the artist's agency. In the absence of a gap between the image and its look, the outward-directedness of looking is only mimicked in the work of visual art. The judiciousness with which the subject is depicted may vouch for the probity and integrity with which an artist regards the referent of his or her work, but it is not that probity itself: it is an artistic representation of an ethical comportment, applying to an artifactual likeness what its creator owes to the referent of that likeness. To speak of an ethics of the moving image is, by comparison, not to speak metaphorically.

The moving image's ethics of looking is not one and the same with the ethics of looking in general. For one thing, the ethics of the moving image cannot be disentangled from the art of the moving image. Shot composition in cinema involves approaching the act of looking with a set of criteria that are more or less extrinsic to perception understood as the gauging of one's surroundings. The act of looking comes to be aligned with the telling of a story whose narrative trajectory the filmmakers know in advance; it subserves the exposition of a truth or a call to arms; or it submits to aesthetic imperatives in its arrangement of the objects inside the frame. In whichever case the act of looking is no longer a simple sensuous exposure to an environment that one can never expect to control fully. Art enters into looking inasmuch as what one sees is mediated by the interests and purposes of a work. In this respect a documentary filmmaker can never eschew art altogether: beauty can be declared a matter of indifference, but the camera's intrusion on the naiveté of looking means that decisions must be made on shot selection and composition that the naked eye as such does not come up against. This is not the skill with which the observant can survey a space and pick out what is relevant to their undertakings. It is the skill not of discriminating among objects within one's visual field, but rather of shaping the visual field as a totality. In this holism it communicates with the modern concept of art, even if it can function as a tool, contributing to a polemical end—alien in kind—to which it is a means.

The artistry that envelops the act of looking in cinema is nevertheless a poor basis for an amoral aestheticism, because the profilmic bodies in the shot are unidentifiable with the figments of an artist's imagination. This self-subsistence of the profilmic is underscored in a documentary wherein the individuals depicted have not assumed roles in a fiction. The documentary, however, is an unilluminating, even misleading argument for this self-subsistence. This is because the credentials for the profilmic's self-subsistence are bound up with the viewer's cognitive transcendence of the image. We believe we know that the body on screen has or at least had a life and reality off screen. The directedness or intentionality of the act of looking is consequently mimicked in the documentary as it is in the representations of a painting or a sculpture. The ethical comportment of looking is not made an affair of the image itself. Sternberg's cinema of spectacle, by contrast, addresses the ethical questions specific to the image.

These are questions that are relatively new to ethics, since they emanate from cinematic fictions. With the advent of film, the image of a person calls for an ethical comportment specific to it as image. The suggestion of fetishism that shrouds Sternberg's work is pertinent here, even if also commonly misinterpreted. For the diagnosis of fetishism to amount to an objection against Sternberg's Dietrich cycle, the peculiarities of the cinematic image of a person have to be neglected. In Sternberg's films the ethical question of what we owe to the image of a person is revisited. That we might owe anything at all to the image of a person is no longer simply because we treat the image as the proxy of the person to whom respect is properly due. The cinematic image, as an image of an actor's characterization, does not easily resolve into a proxy of the person who exists apart from his or her representation. The image comes into its own as worthy of respect. In its independence of the actor whose likeness it captures, it is not a mere thing among things. A person—namely, the fictional character—is present in the image, not just represented by artistic means. An ethics of the moving image is an ethics that is responsive to the demands and obligations that follow from an acknowledgment of these persons endemic to cinema. Sternberg's idolatry of Dietrich is a tribute paid to her characters' images.

This is as much as to say that implicit in Sternberg's cinema of spectacle is an indifference to iconoclasm and a confrontation with the latter's ongoing ramifications for the standing of the phenomenal realm. The ontological constitution of the cinematic likeness, its novelty as an image is misunderstood whenever premodern strictures against artistic reproductions are allowed to determine the way in which the moving image is judged. If Sternberg cuts an unlikely figure as the combatant who squares off against the legacy of Platonism and the Abrahamic religions, it has to be asked what form such a combatant might otherwise be envisaged as taking. The fight for the rehabilitation of the image, if it is not to embroil itself in a performative contradiction (a philosophical defense of the image, for example, cannot help making a concept of the image it purports to defend), has to be by way of pure spectacle.[1] A reclamation of the image need not entail an assertion of the monism of the spectacular, as though Guy Debord and Jean Baudrillard are the inevitable points of orientation for an account of Sternberg's cinema. To appeal the terms of iconoclasm's sentence on the image, it is enough to make room for an appreciation of images in their variety and specificity (reality and transcendence do not have to be collapsed into spectacle).

Why is the moving image and, more especially, Sternberg's cinema cut out for lodging this appeal? To begin with, the epistemic qualities of film's technological reproduction of reality complicate the traditional lay case against the image. The automatism with which the camera records what is before it is at odds with the agency of the liar. Whereas the image-making facility of the camera is by genus at the mercy of the profilmic, the image-making talent of a painter is necessarily subject, in the freedom with which it handles each new object it represents, to doubts over the impartiality of its testimony. The cinematic image, as a class, is epistemologically more robust than the images of premodernity (or the computer-generated images of postmodernity, for that matter). In one respect, what can be said in defense of the moving image can, of course, also be said of Sternberg's cinema: its images enlist their referents in the very act of representations. But what can be said more narrowly of Sternberg's cinema is that the free-floating nature of its spectacle ensures that the cinematic image is not hastily exonerated before the tribunal of the everyday understanding of truth: the image is not rehabilitated to the point that it is assimilated to truth and disappears as image. Depending on the adversary, the image has here in Sternberg's cinema at least some chance of holding its ground precisely as image.

To answer the traditional lay case against the untruthfulness of the image is not, however, to put iconoclasm to rest in its more philosophical and religious motivations. From the vantage point of iconoclasm, the everyday understanding of truth is itself at fault—ensnared as it is in phenomenality, any pardon it might extend to the image is void. The Platonic charge against the image is that it distorts and adulterates what it is imputed to depict; the Abrahamic charge is that it usurps the place of God.[2] What the image, according to Plato, fails to depict is the idea, and it fails not only because it falls short in attempting to reproduce its phenomenal model, but also because this phenomenal model is for its part likewise an image, which falls short in attempting to reproduce the idea. What justifies the destruction of the image, from the point of view of the doctrine of God's transcendence, is that simply as phenomenon the image cannot be worshipped without a blasphemous repudiation of the reverence that is due to the one true God. The two charges against the image—one epistemological, the other theological—by no means convert into each other. The practical iconoclasm that has followed from them is by necessity an unfinished business. So long as we perceive with the senses, we remain before the corrupt images of ideas that parade against the wall of Plato's cave, and so long as the shattering of images has its rationale in the correcting of the religious practice of others, there is no dearth of objects before which the impious might bow down in adoration.

What renders the image traditionally vulnerable to the Platonic and Abrahamic charges is its referentiality. The image points beyond itself and hence is involved in its own operation of transcendence. It points elsewhere but is insufficiently radical in its conception of the transcendent: in the self-denial whereby it generates its reference, it never goes so far as to deny phenomenality en masse. The simple negation of the image is the culmination of an immanent process of self-effacement before the referent—every image, one might be tempted to say, flirts with the iconoclasm in which it is both realized and destroyed. In the case of cinematic fictions, it is nevertheless debatable whether their images point beyond themselves and press a claim to transcendence that Platonism and Abrahamic iconoclasm cannot help deeming inadequate. A real person is not behind, but within the image. Sternberg's images, for instance, do not refer to a world that exists separately from them and yet they do not cease to be images—and not just in the Platonic sense in which every phenomenon is an image of its idea. They are images because they are looks. What we see is the look that Sternberg has made from the objects in front of the camera rather than these objects themselves. The profilmic phenomenal world in its three-dimensionality is not the fuller truth of which the cinematic image is a vitiated representation. Were we able to inspect the objects composing a given shot from angles and positions not adopted by the filmmaker, we would obtain a garbled rather than clearer impression of the work per se (which is not to deny that we would know more about the *making* of the film).

Sternberg's cinema discovers a transcendence internal to the image. It would be wrong to think of this as a mimicking of transcendence along the lines of the mimicking of the directedness of the look in painting and sculpture. It would also be wrong to discern here an artist's demonic aping of the divine act of creation, as though the self-contained universe of the cinematic image amounts to an adjuration and mocking miniature of the world that is the work of God. This is because the transcendence internal to the image is not a human artifact: the image openly displays the limits of the filmmaker's artistic agency in the presence of the profilmic. The image transcends itself only to return to itself, for that which is more than image exists only as image. Cinematic fiction sublates the profilmic, annulling it in favor of what it creates from it and yet preserving it but only inasmuch as it cannot create without it. The fictional persons who move within the frame have no life outside it.[3]

What follows from this new species of image is a disabling or, at least, a mitigating of certain criticisms of phenomenality. Ethics, inasmuch as it has been defined by a commitment to the exceptionalism of persons among material objects, here has to linger with the image if it is to acknowledge the transcendence proper to the visible. To destroy the image, as iconoclasm enjoins, is not to free the transcendence of the person, but rather to smash it. Even if the cinema of fantasy that Georges Méliès inaugurated did not reverse the sentence that the West has passed on materiality as a whole, these films nonetheless provide a small sanctuary within which matter need not fear being judged against a transcendence external to it and thereby found wanting. The cinematic image of a fictional character is the person become artifact. In his close-ups of Dietrich's characters, Sternberg affords a glimpse into the post-Anthropocene utopia that awaits material things after millennia of persecution.

If there is an ethics to Sternberg's cinema, it is thus not just a case of "doing right" by his star's appearance. The standing of materiality is at issue. Seeing this face necessitates not looking beyond it. By not canceling itself out, the image presses the claim of its own materiality for a recognition of the transcendence specific and internal to it as artifact. The exceptionalism of the person is accordingly not won at the price of materiality in general—it is an act of generosity on the part of the face toward things if it makes itself into an image and no more than an image. Captured by the camera, the face does not dissolve into the mere thingliness of the image's materiality and hence exerts a liberating pressure on this materiality even as it remains fully and—in *The Devil Is a Woman*, if not earlier—only visible. It is a one-sided assessment of Sternberg's images that notes simply the objectification of his star, because there simultaneously takes place in this hypostasis a corresponding movement on the part of matter in the opposite direction. As mere images, the various faces of Dietrich's characters give themselves up to be contemplated in their materiality and not in spite of it. By contrast, Levinas's iconoclastic phenomenology maintains that the face cannot be seen at all, that what is seen in place of it is never a face.[4] Levinas's elevation of the face corresponds to and depends upon a denigration of the visibility of the nontranscendent. This is ethics as a zero-sum game.

Levinas conflates the Platonic and Abrahamic charges in "Reality and Its Shadow" (1948) when he invokes the monotheistic proscription of images in order to denounce the idolatry of all representational art, irrespective of the object it professes to portray and the comportment that is adopted in relation to it.[5] In this he exemplifies the difficulty that the image has in gaining a fair hearing. The odds are stacked against it because the image aggravates the faults for which materiality is indicted by both Platonism and the Abrahamic religions. Whereas matter's deficiency, according to Plato, is that it is inadequately itself (its idea), the failing of materiality that conversely bears out the religious proscription of images is that it is too much itself (the immanent in contradistinction from the transcendent). For Levinas, the image is ethically most at fault when it presumes to render visible the essentially invisible face. This substitution of the human face for the transcendent deity of the proscription of images approaches, in its own way, the very idolatry that Exodus 20:4–5 prohibits. The substitution is consistent, however, with Genesis 1:26–27 inasmuch as God, by creating human beings in his image, creates a being that is necessarily also unimaginable. And yet it does not follow that the religious proscription of images stretches to representations of the human, given that to be human is to be an image. An image of a human being is an image of an image; it is a representation of a representation of the unrepresentable. What the ethics of the image requires is a redemptive acknowledgment of the image's materiality, for to look beyond the image to the transcendent is not to see the image at all.

There is of course no point in pretending that the ethics in Sternberg's handling of images recovers him for the company of the wholesome, just as there is no good reason to believe that an ethics specific to the moving image must coexist with a horror or even just a sober rejection of all forms of depravity. The ethical multivalence of Sternberg's cinema is at its most glaring in *The Shanghai Gesture* (1941), an adaptation of John Colton's 1926 play of the same name. In an early scene that Debord was to include in his film *The Society of the Spectacle* (1974), Poppy (Gene Tierney) addresses the camera as she surveys the luxurious gambling den watched over by "Mother" Gin Sling (Ona Munson):

POPPY. The other places are like kindergartens compared with this. (*closing her eyes with the intensity of her enjoyment*) It smells so incredibly evil. I didn't think such a place existed except in my own imagination. It has a ghastly familiarity like a half-remembered dream. (*looking now directly into the camera*) Anything could happen here, any moment.

It is a magnificent shot and the remainder of the film never figures out how it might fulfill the promise it contains. By looking the viewer straight in the eye, Gene Tierney issues an invitation to evil. The space in which anything could happen is the nonspace that Tierney shares with the viewer. The viewer, not knowing how to take up the offer, resigns the film to its awkwardly melodramatic narrative. Tierney never addresses the camera again in this way, and the poise and self-command with which she here faces the viewer quickly desert her as her characterization proceeds to disintegrate into querulous tantrums and pouting quite unlike anything in Dietrich's performances for Sternberg. True evil, as the shot suggests and as it relates to the cinematic image in its specificity, is an affair of the viewer's interaction with the profilmic. Whenever the viewer cannot help declining Gene Tierney's invitation to experience together evil in all its voluptuousness, the film settles for a makeshift in the shape of the content of the image. As ravishing as Keye Luke's murals for the film's finale are, the banquet scene's cascade of revelations—the curtains pulled aside to show the caged women suspended outside in advance of being auctioned off to the owners of so-called flower boats, "Mother" Gin Sling's announcement that she was the lover that Poppy's father had married only to abandon, and then the pot-boiler twist that in ruining Poppy in her quest to exact revenge on her erstwhile husband "Mother" Gin Sling has unawares ruined her own daughter—does not manage to implicate the viewer in its fiction.[6] The question of the ethics of the look is left dormant.

Gene Tierney's exhortation to the viewer to come share with her the intoxicating smell of evil—sensorially unavailable so long as the viewer tarries in front of the screen—cites as well as disavows the theatrical practice of direct audience address. A close-up, while it isolates an actor from the ensemble and the interactions

FIGURE C.1. "Anything could happen here, any moment": glancing briefly into the camera, Gene Tierney as Poppy asks for the audience's collusion rather than sympathy in *The Shanghai Gesture* (dir. Josef von Sternberg, Arnold Pressburger Films, 1941).

that constitute the narrative, can never break the fourth wall in earnest, since that which in the theater is a matter of a convention and a mode of reception becomes, in cinema, a genuine physical division because the audience and the cast do not occupy the same time and space. There can only ever be a playing at direct audience address even as the face within the close-up assumes a size to dominate the viewer's visual field and even as the viewer can stare unflinchingly into the actor's eyes. The close-up does not so much reference the fact of the common world in which the illusion of a fiction is otherwise being contrived as it declares that this common world does not exist.[7] The fourth wall that is the cinematic medium itself is more durable than the sides of the bottles in which djinn are imprisoned. This impregnability of the seal enclosing a cinematic fiction alters the meaning of direct audience address because it bears on the relationship between actor and role. Whereas in the theater an actor is able momentarily (and possibly unprofessionally) to leave his or her role behind to communicate directly with the audience within the time and space that they share, in film an actor remains on the side of the fiction, continuing ineluctably within its particular time and space notwithstanding all the show of a heart-to-heart with the viewer. Sternberg's close-ups of Dietrich do not extricate from whatever role she happens to be playing the professional actor born in Berlin in 1901. They can make the role shudder as it starts to oscillate in the presence of the Dietrich persona, but the latter is only another cinematic fiction rather than a flesh-and-blood human being with whom the audience coexists in the one confined time and space. And that this persona is as much Sternberg's as Dietrich's, a denizen of the lighting systems and camera angles to which he knew to confine her, might be argued on the basis of the fitfulness with which it is sighted in Dietrich's post-Sternberg cinematic appearances. In *The Shanghai Gesture* it is Gene Tierney-as-Poppy who summons the viewer to a celebration of evil. She cannot step out of her role, although she can establish a line of sight between her role and the viewer in front of the screen: we are addressed by an image that has no reality outside the fiction.

The image represents Gene Tierney, and without in any way fudging the depiction, it also represents someone else. It exhibits the profilmic body that was Gene Tierney, and in the very act of this exhibition it engenders the image of the character of Poppy as realized by Tierney. As a cinematic image, Poppy solidifies in a henceforth memorialized time and space that Tierney occupied only in passing. The cinematic recording of a production doubles the constructivism whereby actors in a theater, always only ever provisionally and in collusion with an audience, fashion a time and space different from the time and space of the performance. It doubles this constructivism by objectifying it, so to speak, and dehumanizing it. The alternative here-and-now of the fiction that in the theater rubs up against the time and space of the performance surrenders this contact with the present when it stands over and against it as nothing more than the present screening of a cinematic artifact datable to the past. For it to able to leave behind the reality prevailing in the auditorium during a screening, a film has other resources at its disposal than the theater's act of collective make-believe, because the hegemonic grip of the present is loosened by the cinema's injection of a dose of the past. Film substantializes the alternative time and space of fiction, lending heft to the characters that populate it. The characterization acquires an independence of the actor who survives the recording but who ages and dies before the film in question can be definitively said to have been screened for the last time. What looks back from the image, what asserts its difference from a mere thing, is the character in his or her ascendancy over the role's profilmic vehicle.

Here a living person is in the image as opposed to the image being of a living person. The case of the cinematic image of a fictional character differs from the sitter of a photographic portrait whose appearance is preserved by the metaphorical embalming fluids of the medium, like an insect captured in amber. Having no life apart from the image, the character cannot be said to live on in the image in a reduced and constrained form. The image is the character's element. It does not eternalize the character, abstracting it from time and space, so much as provide it with the time and space in which it can first exist. Likewise, what movement there is to the moving image does not follow on behind the movement of the character, aiming to reproduce it—the character moves with the image and as the image. The traditional ethics that transcend the image toward the person meets here with nothing that it can pretend is deserving of respect, for there is no reality to the fictional character separate from the image. An ethics of the moving image of fictional characters is an ethics that has made its peace with the materiality of real people and with materiality as such. It is an ethics of the look. It neither negates what it sees in the name of an affirmation of the invisible nor degrades what it sees to a mere object for being visible at all. (As much as these two approaches to the act of looking define themselves in opposition to each other, they also corroborate each other in their shared evaluation of the reified character of the visible.)

For Sternberg, to film is to accord the visible its due; it is to treat visibility not as a given, but as a task and duty to which the filmmaker must rise. In *The Docks of New York* (1928), after Mae (Betty Compson) is pulled unconscious from the waters in which she had sought to drown, she comes to life as an image. Everything around her is white and it colludes with the whiteness of her skin and hair to bring her to visibility: the smoke of her cigarette, the paint on the wrought iron bedstead and on the wall behind her, her nightgown no less than the sheets are all part and parcel of her image. This is not a virginal whiteness, but exasperation and exhausted bemusement as whiteness, as values that become visible in whiteness and by means of which whiteness can become visible afresh. Sternberg makes Mae stand out not from the things surrounding her but with them. Attending to the visibility of the person here means attending to the materiality of everything contained within the frame. (To remark the objectification involved in a so-called glamor shot and not the accompanying movement in the opposite direction on the part of the non-human content of the image is one-sided.)

Light gives life to the image and also takes it away. In *The Saga of Anatahan* (1953), the last film Sternberg directed, the living soldiers who return to Japan after the end of the Second World War are greeted by a bank of photographers' flash bulbs on the airport apron. Against a back-projection of a four-engine turbo-prop airliner, the soldiers walk toward the camera between two lines of uniformed men and flit repeatedly, if but momentarily out of sight because of the white-out wrought by the photographers' flashes (what enables the photograph disables the film). These disruptions of visibility mark their transition back into Japanese society following years spent on Anatahan in the Northern Mariana Islands, cut off from the outside world and its historical reckoning: the photographers' flashes in effect translate the blinking of eyes that are new to the light of day after an extended sojourn in the underworld. The end of the film shows the characters who died on Anatahan also returning to Japan. Whereas the living walked toward the camera and then passed it to its left, looking all the while beyond it, presumably to the cheering crowd of family members awaiting them and to whom they could be taken to smile in recognition, the dead walk directly up to the camera, staring dolefully into it. The photographers do not fire their bulbs in order to capture their likenesses. The only light that illuminates them is restricted to the immediate foreground of the camera. Emerging from the shadows in which the two lines of uniformed men are preserved as silhouettes, they do not enter the light of a world that pretends to exist beyond the film's fiction, for they have no lives to which they might return on the Japanese mainland—they are resolutely creatures of the converted Kyoto studio in which Sternberg shot the film. However much the narrative of *The Saga of Anatahan* might skirt the scabrous realism of the human condition that Freud's speculative scenario of the primal horde and William Golding's *Lord of the Flies* (1954) often are read as claiming for themselves, Sternberg's film of a struggle to the death over a woman never suppresses the artifice of the circumstances of its production. The trees of the tropical island on which it is set glisten with the aluminum paint with which Sternberg had sprayed them, as though what is here to pass for nature in its savage state should not be confidently distinguished from a discarded Dietrich headdress. A tree, as far as Sternberg is concerned, cannot properly show itself under studio lighting as a tree unless it arrays itself with the requisite mineral properties.

In Sternberg's cinema being and doing are subordinate to gesture. A tree cannot be left to be a tree: it has to perform. In the microcosm of his studio shoots the artifice and suspended state of fiction are embraced rather than disavowed, and that which elsewhere might be a matter of mechanical laws becomes expressive. This expressiveness is not the same as the communication of intelligible content. It is more a case of the self-consciousness the presence of a camera induces in the profilmic, whether animate or inanimate. An image distinct from a documentary reproduction of the real is generated. Making a show of its visibility, the profilmic compensates for the subartistic aspect of cinematic representation, for what the act of filming lacks in individual expressiveness by virtue of the technological automatism with which it records what is before the camera, the bodies, faces, and objects in Sternberg's work see fit to supply. An action that does not build itself up into a gesture, that does not pause in the pursuit of its goal to consider its own image is an action that leaves the filmmaker in the lurch regarding the competition with representational art.

Dietrich, of course, is Sternberg's greatest collaborator in the invention of gestures. There is a deliberateness to her movements that announces the preparation of a gesture, its execution, and the body's release from the act of execution. She slows proceedings down to give the image the time it needs to crystallize. But Dietrich by no means monopolizes the histrionic expressiveness of Sternberg's cinema. A corporeal surrealism creeps in at various junctures. In *Crime and Punishment* (1935), for instance, during one of the interrogation scenes Raskolnikov (Peter Lorre) self-importantly puts his foot up a chair and Porfiry (Edward Arnold) reaches over and tickles him gently on the inside of his right knee to prompt him to remove it. The action calls attention to itself because of the eccentricity with which it goes about achieving its purpose. Underlining by its singularity the singularity of the moment in which it occurs, it is also unlike the gestures that compose a people's inherited set of bodily reflexes. The Sternbergian gesture, in its suspension of both instrumental rationality and the laws of its environment, verges on the magical. When Larry Semon descends the staircase to the bar in *Underworld* (1927), the crispness and theatricality of the presentational style with which he doffs his hat frame and merge with the magic trick wherein he flings his hat from him only for it to return to him like a boomerang. The enchantment of gestures is not something to which the characters themselves are insusceptible. It is understandable that Dietrich's Concha would run off with the bullfighter Morenito (Don Alvarado), for when she praises him, he snaps his fingers and rolls his eyes in laconic self-deprecation: the masculinity of the gesture's message is sublated by the physical artistry that coins and enacts the gesture. Sternberg's is a cinema that favors those who experiment with expression—they are the natives of the image.

Sternberg's images are necessarily and intractably collaborations. Products of the studio system, his films were not shot on the sly, without the knowledge of the persons who appear in them. The participants pose for the camera and are put into poses with an eye to their technological reproduction. They show themselves, but inasmuch as what they show are characters in a work of fiction, they also do not show themselves: the image simultaneously reveals and conceals, thickening into a reality of its own that is a collective imagining rather than one man's fantasy. For the eight years during which Sternberg enjoyed Paramount's support, he was to make films in which all manner of people, every variety of prop, and even the seasons and climates conspired with him to create images that peeled off from the surrounding reality. Sternberg's Hollywood was a moment of cooperative dreaming in which inanimate matter and light itself were swept up. The films are spectacles because they insist on their independence as fictions. This is likewise an independence from the spectator whose gaze can never trouble the temporally congealed surface of the cinematic image. The inhabitants of these spectacles are the recipients of Sternberg's care. He attends to their image. The moralism of his attention consists in the cultivation of the visibility that bides its time in the profilmic as a promise of another form of life rather than being simply given with it. It is not a promise that a director might one-sidedly impose. If the cinematic image is essentially a spectacle because it presents the viewer with a reality that, in being past, no longer admits of intervention, it nonetheless harbors within itself its own set of moral tasks and imperatives. Where the image does not refer beyond itself, where the image is furthermore made of real people, a responsibility acknowledged toward fictional characters will take the shape of a vigilance regarding the thickness and visibility of the image as image. Aestheticism does not do justice to Sternberg's engagement with bringing out the alternative earths with which he knew the profilmic to be swollen. His cinema pays heed to the world's will to break free of itself, to disgorge itself of its possible Marlenes.

Notes

1. Béla Balázs, "Der sichtbare Mensch" in id., *Theory of the Film: Character and Growth of a New Art*, trans. Edith Bone (New York: Dover, 1970), 45. For a defense of the universalism of a limited set of facial expressions, see Paul Ekman, Wallace V. Friesen, and Phoebe Ellsworth, "What Are the Similarities and Differences in Facial Behavior across Cultures?" in id., *Emotion in the Human Face: Guidelines for Research and an Integration of Findings* (New York: Pergamon, 1972), 153–67.

2. Dietrich's own account of Sternberg's reliance on counting in *Morocco* is relayed in Peter Bogdanovich, *Who the Devil Made It* (New York: Ballantine, 1997), 238.

3. Josef von Sternberg, *Fun in a Chinese Laundry* (London: Secker & Warburg, 1966), 96–97.

4. Ibid., 102.

5. Quoted in Tom Flinn, "Joe, Where Are You? (Marlene Dietrich)," *Velvet Light Trap* 6 (Fall 1972): 17. Cf. the remark on this well-known quotation in E. Ann Kaplan, *Women and Film: Both Sides of the Camera* (New York: Methuen, 1983), 52: "As a result of this stance, Von Sternberg's films narcissistically eliminate real consideration of his heroines or their points of view." I will argue that, on the contrary, an elimination of Dietrich's otherness and independence would have injured Sternberg's prospects of seeing his own autonomy in her image (this is not to imply that Sternberg's relationship to Dietrich amounts to anything like an unproblematic illustration of Hegel's theory of recognition).

6. For a discussion of Dietrich's accent, see Allan Bell, "Falling in Love Again and Again: Marlene Dietrich and the Iconization of Non-Native English," *Journal of Sociolinguistics* 15, no. 5 (November 1, 2011): 627–56. Bell analyzes the impersonations by Carol Channing and

Madeline Kahn, noting how they incorporate stereotypically German pronunciations that are nonetheless missing from Dietrich's sung English (647).

7. The overarching narrative admittedly struggles to congeal. In the later scene when Tom Brown and Amy Jolly declare their love for each other, a mirror is used to affirm a distance between them. See the admirable analysis in Carole Zucker, *The Idea of the Image: Josef von Sternberg's Dietrich Films* (Cranbury, NJ: Associated University Press, 1988), 39: "It is not clear exactly where Brown is in relation to Amy within the co-ordinates of the frame; what is unambiguously true is that they are not together. The enigmatic spatial referents in this shot are compounded by the communication of Brown and Amy through the medium of the mirror. The fact that he never enters the frame (until after this interchange) and that she does not leave it is decisive—they prefer to address disembodied reflections at this most crucial moment in their romance."

8. Cf. the analysis of the set design in *The Blue Angel* in Siegfried Kracauer, *From Caligari to Hitler: A Psychological History of the German Film* (Princeton, NJ: Princeton University Press, 1947), 217: "The persistent interference of mute objects reveals the whole milieu as a scene of loosened instincts. Perfect conductors, these objects transmit Jannings' delayed passion as well as the waves of sexual excitement emanating from Lola Lola." Disorder is not intrinsically and uniquely sexual: Kracauer passes too swiftly from the license that Sternberg's mute objects, by their puncturing of the coherence and orderliness of narrative, extend not only to the instincts.

9. See also the insightful discussion in Andrea Weiss, *Vampires and Violets: Lesbians in Film* (London: Cape, 1992), 34–35: "Amy Jolly's performance [. . .] is rendered in point of view shots intercut with the two contending male characters. Yet when her song is finished and she steps over the railing separating performer and audience, the image becomes a tableau. When Amy Jolly looks at the woman at the table, she quickly lowers her eyes to take in the entire body—to 'look her over'; Amy Jolly then turns away and hesitates before looking at her again. The sexual impulses are strong in this gesture, impulses that are not diffused or choked by point of view shots or audience cutaway shots. Dietrich's gaze remains intact."

10. Laura Mulvey, *Visual and Other Pleasures* (New York: Palgrave, 1989), 22. See also the collective statement by the editors of *Cahiers du Cinéma*, "*Morocco*, de Josef von Sternberg," *Cahiers du Cinéma* 225 (November–December 1970): 5–13. The authors' interpretation of Dietrich as a fetish entails a similar neglect of her agency and autonomy. Gaylyn Studlar's *In the Realm of Pleasure: Von Sternberg, Dietrich, and the Masochistic Aesthetic* (New York: Columbia University Press, 1988) is a further example of this approach.

11. Cf. the analysis of Dreyer's close-ups of Falconetti in Michael Tawa, *Agencies of the Frame: Tectonic Strategies in Cinema and Architecture* (Newcastle upon Tyne: Cambridge Scholars, 2011), 110: "It is in fact a looking out for the look of the Other which subverts the violating and captivating power of the gaze."

12. G. W. F. Hegel, *Aesthetics*, trans. T. M. Knox (Oxford: Clarendon Press, 1975), 153–54.

13. Jean Mitry, *The Aesthetics and Psychology of the Cinema*, trans. Christopher King (Bloomington: Indiana University Press, 1997), 162.

14. Jack Smith, "Belated Appreciation of V. S.," *Film Culture* 31 (1963–64): 5.

15. James Naremore, *Acting in the Cinema* (Berkeley: University of California Press, 1988), 131. On the fluidity with which she shifts between her commitment to her characterization within a given film and the maintenance of her star persona's narrative autonomy, see also 156: "Dietrich plays her part with an alternating conviction and irony that few American actors then or now would attempt."

16. Sternberg, *Fun in a Chinese Laundry*, 72.

17. Ibid., 313.

18. *Dishonored* is not without its admirers. Pascal Mérigeau, for instance, praising its richness of invention and internal coherence as well as its handling of ambient sound and music, considers it "certainly one of the most 'complete' of Sternberg's films." See Pascal Mérigeau, *Josef von Sternberg* (Paris: Edilig, 1983), 73.

19. Sergei Eisenstein, "A Course in Treatment," in *Film Form: Essays in Film Theory*, ed. and trans. Jay Leyda (London: Dennis Dobson, 1951), 106.

1 *SHANGHAI EXPRESS*: MAKING ROOM FOR FAITH IN APPEARANCES

1. Jean-Luc Nancy, *Philosophical Chronicles*, trans. Franson Manjali (New York: Fordham University Press, 2008), 69. Nancy's querying of the knowability of the face *as seen* recalls Emmanuel Levinas's writings on the ethics of images of the human, although it does not lead him to adopt the latter's iconoclasm. (The issue of the ethics of Sternberg's images will be addressed in the Conclusion.)

2. Jules Furthman, *Shanghai Express* in id., Morocco *and* Shanghai Express: *Two Films by Josef von Sternberg* (New York: Simon and Schuster, 1973), 129–31. The use of italics for dialogue follows the published shooting script. My comments on Furthman's screenplay are comments on the dialogue as contained in the shooting script.

3. 1 Corinthians 13:12. Quotations from the Bible are from the authorized King James version of 1611.

4. Cf. the reading of the station reconciliation scene in Peter Wollen, *Signs and Meaning in the Cinema* (London: British Film Institute, 1998), 147. For Wollen, this is an occasion "on which woman is—rather pathetically—put back in her place." Such an interpretation entails neglecting the conditions on which Shanghai Lily declares a reconciliation could come to pass: domestication is not in the cards. As though to quash the idea that Shanghai Lily was also on a journey of moral renewal as she traveled from Peking to Shanghai, she wears in the final scene the same ensemble of glamorized disreputableness in which she boarded the train (and by an optical illusion, because of where he stands facing her on the other side of a jeweler's shop window, the man with whom she is to be reconciled appears to have donned a string of pearls).

5. 2 Corinthians 5:7.

6. Immanuel Kant, *Critique of the Power of Judgment*, trans. Paul Guyer and Eric Matthews (Cambridge: Cambridge University Press, 2000), 5: 207–9.

7. Furthman, *Shanghai Express*, 64.

8. Ibid., 71.

9. Ibid., 63.

10. Ibid., 112.

11. Whatever Asianness the film's first audiences might have been willing to ascribe to Chang was surely a matter of the Swedish-American actor Warner Oland's numerous preceding outings as Fu Manchu and Charlie Chan (for Paramount and Fox, respectively).

12. Gina Marchetti, *Romance and the "Yellow Peril": Race, Sex, and Discursive Strategies in Hollywood Fiction* (Berkeley: University of California Press, 1993), 61.

13. That Ona Munson, best known for her role as the brothel madam Belle Watling in *Gone with the Wind* (1939), wears yellowface in Sternberg's *The Shanghai Gesture* (1941) is a regrettable

lapse in judgment, which the camp excess of the character's elaborate, lacquered hairpieces—in themselves a welcome resurgence of Sternberg's visual bravura after his Columbia productions—merely aggravates, resulting in racist kitsch.

14. Whatever insult might be ascribed to his setting off of Keeler's homeliness against Dietrich's glamour and mystery Berkeley more than makes amends for by the star treatment he gives Keeler in his delirious and enchanting visualization of another Al Dubin and Harry Warren song, "I Only Have Eyes for You" in *Dames* (1934): the modesty and geniality of Keeler's face are the internal resistance to the lavishness of Berkeley's homage, allowing him to go further and further without cloying his audience.

15. Sternberg, *Fun in a Chinese Laundry*, 325.

16. However intense and visceral one's response to the images in a horror movie, the cinematic experience is not absolute but rather doubled by its negation: these are images that are conceived to be seen in order not to be seen. When judged in conjunction with the viewer response to which it aspires, the horror movie can be classified a variation on the abstract film. Both belong to a self-effacing, ironic cinema because both, albeit in different ways, draw back from cinema's technological possibility of a contemplation of the profilmic in its existential thickness. The viewer who averts his or her gaze from the organisms reproduced on screen while watching a horror movie—and not to avert one's gaze is to respond ironically to an ironic genre—resembles the abstract director who in the making of his or her films disavows the putatively extracinematic.

17. Furthman, *Shanghai Express*, 69–70.

18. Ibid., 91.

19. Ibid., 136.

20. Ibid., 126.

21. Taking issue with Carole Zucker's interpretation of this shot, Catherine Constable denies that the disruptiveness of the image has to do with Dietrich's transcendence of her role. See Catherine Constable, *Thinking in Images: Film Theory, Feminist Philosophy and Marlene Dietrich* (London: BFI, 2005), 152: "Zucker's reading of the medium close-up of Dietrich's face as a star moment does not address the content of the shot. This is unfortunate because the lighting set-up might be seen to support her argument. The placing of a key light in line with Dietrich's forehead as she gazes upwards etches out her prominent cheekbones, sculpting her face into the familiar contours of her star image. However, the expression on her face does not conform to the sculpted beauty of a star moment. Indeed, the intensity with which Lily gazes up at Doc has the effect of making her look somewhat haggard." Cf. the famous description of the kiss in Marcel Proust, *The Guermantes Way*, trans. Mark Treharne (London: Penguin, 2002), 362–63: "As my mouth began to move towards the cheeks my eyes had led it to want to kiss, my eyes changed position and saw different cheeks; the neck, observed at closer range and as if through a magnifying glass, became coarse-grained and showed a sturdiness which altered the character of the face." Disillusionment, of course, does not guarantee that one judges correctly.

22. Gilles Deleuze, *Cinema 1: The Movement-Image*, trans. Hugh Tomlinson and Barbara Habberjam (London: Bloomsbury, 2013), 104–6.

23. Alfred Baeumler, *Das Irrationalitätsproblem in der Ästhetik und Logik des 18. Jahrhunderts bis zur* Kritik der Urteilskraft (Darmstadt: Wissenschaftliche Buchgesellschaft, 1967).

1. In its open partisanship for an adulteress, Sternberg's *mise-en-scène* is exemplary of the independence of expression—for instance, in relation to a Code-compliant script—by which *Cahiers du Cinéma* identified the auteurs among Hollywood directors. For an analysis of the sequence, see Bill Nichols, *Ideology and the Image* (Bloomington: Indiana University Press, 1981), 116–19. Whereas Lee Garmes had been the cinematographer on Sternberg's four previous films at Paramount, Bert Glennon shot *Blonde Venus*, resuming a collaboration that began with *Underworld*.

2. Cf. Stanley Cavell, *Contesting Tears: The Hollywood Melodrama of the Unknown Woman* (Chicago: University of Chicago Press, 1996), 15: "An outstanding question about *Blonde Venus* is why the woman returns to the marriage—how Marlene Dietrich could, never more attractive and independent than here, and even for the sake of her child, credibly return to conjugal life with that ordinary, vindictive, stuffed shirt. (It is Herbert Marshall for whom she leaves Cary Grant. Imagine.) It makes sense of the events to say: she has judged the world she has seen, and she has seen much of it, to be second-rate, one whose unnecessary stinginess with happiness she can do nothing to improve. But her son has, even in such a world, a chance to do something, with a mother like her to teach him what men and women can be like." If those who cannot, teach, it can only be because they have not taken to heart the world's lesson regarding its stinginess with happiness.

3. Cf. Robin Wood, "Venus de Marlene," *Film Comment* 14, no. 2 (March–April 1978): 58–63. For Wood, the bartender admits "his terror of *real* gorillas" (61) by stuttering uncontrollably. But this is to apply ingenuity in the service of not getting a joke (the bartender also stutters when he subsequently answers an unrelated question from Taxi).

4. See Sianne Ngai, "Black Venus, *Blonde Venus*" in *Bad Modernisms*, eds. Douglas Mao and Rebecca L. Walkowitz (Durham, NC: Duke University Press, 2006), 145–78. Tania Modleski comparably charges the "Hot Voodoo" sequence with racism without considering its self-mockery and irony in the handling of racist stereotypes. See the discussion in Tania Modleski, *Feminism Without Women: Culture and Criticism in a "Postfeminist" Age* (Abingdon: Routledge, 1991), 127–29.

5. *Der Blaue Engel: Die Drehbuchentwürfe*, eds. Luise Dirscherl and Gunther Nickel (St. Ingbert: Röhrig, 2000), 86, 173–74, and 323–27. The song she "murders" is Schubert's "Ständchen."

6. This is generalized into a vocational trait in Marlene Dietrich, *My Life*, trans. Salvator Attanasio (London: Weidenfeld and Nicolson, 1989), 140: "Artists are optimistic; they are born so they can be saved by unexpected miracles."

7. Ernst Bloch, *Traces*, trans. Anthony A. Nassar (Stanford, CA: Stanford University Press, 2006), 158. But see also Sternberg's letter of December 5, 1967 in Frieda Grafe, *Aus dem Off: Zum Kino in den Sechzigern* (Berlin: Brinkmann & Bose, 2003), 167–68, where in response to Grafe's notice in *Die Zeit* (no. 48) on his autobiography he strenuously denies the relevance of Judaism to the story of his life.

8. Jorge Luis Borges, "The Wall and the Books," trans. James E. Irby in id., *Labyrinths: Selected Stories and Other Writings* (New York: New Directions, 1964), 188.

9. Peter Baxter, *Just Watch!: Sternberg, Paramount and America* (London: British Film Institute, 1993), 165.

10. Silvia Bovenschen, "Is There a Feminine Aesthetic?" trans. Beth Weckmueller, *New German Critique* 10 (Winter 1977): 129–30. Maria Riva also testifies to the exactitude of her mother's stage persona. See Maria Riva, *Marlene Dietrich: By Her Daughter* (London: Bloomsbury, 1992), 713: "Being the innate, trainable soldier that she was, the structure of her performances never varied. Even when she was drunk, one could set one's stopwatch by when an arm would lift, a special pause would occur, a look punctuate a meaning of a lyric, a measured silence, a lowering of the head. With her amazing discipline, she Xeroxed her performance, night after night, year after year."

11. Elfriede Jelinek, "Das zweite Gesicht," *Die Zeit* (May 15, 1992): 75–76. The epigraph for this chapter is drawn from this text (76). Dwelling on Dietrich's inassimilability to the Third Reich's image of submissive womanhood, Jelinek, like Bovenschen, credits Dietrich's act with an independence that amounts to far more than the passing and specious resistance of the sexual tease.

12. Andrew Sarris, *The Films of Josef von Sternberg* (New York: The Museum of Modern Art, 1966), 36.

13. Lea Jacobs, *The Wages of Sin: Censorship and the Fallen Woman Film 1928–1942* (Madison: University of Wisconsin Press, 1991), 105. Peter Baxter's *Just Watch!: Sternberg, Paramount and America* offers a comprehensive reconstruction of the studio's supervision of the drafting process for *Blonde Venus*.

14. Jacobs, *The Wages of Sin*, 85.

15. Molly Haskell, *From Reverence to Rape: The Treatment of Women in the Movies* (New York: Holt, Rinehart and Winston, 1973), 98.

16. Peter Baxter, "The Birth of *Venus*," *Wide Angle: A Film Quarterly of Theory, Criticism, and Practice* 10, no. 1 (1988): 11: "The Hollywood cinema struggled so with the problem of conceptualizing the world in which it existed, because it was itself a part of the system that had caused that world to edge toward the abyss, and it had nothing with which to comprehend the situation save the desperate ability to fantasize." For all the pitilessness of its handling of the theme of a mother whose child is torn away from her, Sternberg's earlier *The Case of Lena Smith* (1929), of which only a four-minute fragment has survived, is not a counterexample to Baxter's generalization, for the misery that the film does not flinch in depicting was expatriated from the New York of Samuel Ornitz's original story to the Austro-Hungarian Empire of Jules Furthman's final script—and Sternberg's own childhood. See Alexander Horwath and Michael Omasta (eds.), *Josef von Sternberg: The Case of Lena Smith* (Vienna: Synema, 2007).

3 *THE SCARLET EMPRESS*: HISTORY AS FARCE

1. See, for instance, Peter Baxter, *Just Watch!: Sternberg, Paramount and America*, 189: "In order to make *The Scarlet Empress* and *The Devil Is a Woman*, he took advantage of the corporate disarray into which Paramount had been sliding during 1932, when its most experienced executives were ousted and the company left bereft of a coherent management."

2. Quoted in Herman G. Weinberg, *Josef von Sternberg: A Critical Study* (New York: E. P. Dutton, 1967), 130.

3. Joseph Conrad, "Preface" to *The Nigger of the "Narcissus"* (Oxford: Oxford University Press, 1984), xxxix.

4. Philip Jenkinson, "Von Sternberg's Last Interview," *Film Culture* 76 (1992): 40–43.

5. Dissatisfied with the set-ups during the shooting of *The Song of Songs*, Dietrich infamously appealed via a microphone to the darkened recesses of the studio: "Jo, where are you?"

6. See her daughter's description of her appearance in Maria Riva, *Marlene Dietrich*, 272: "When she finally did her first scene in *The Scarlet Empress*, she played it so 'wide-eyed innocence,' with so many shy curtseys and bobbings, that she looked like the village idiot dressed in a bassinet."

7. See also the analysis of the film's early scenes in Carole Zucker, *The Idea of the Image: Josef von Sternberg's Dietrich Films*, 118–19. According to Zucker, there is no attempt to have Dietrich pass for a young girl: not wearing makeup that might conceal her age, Dietrich cites other women who have played girls in film, jumping up and down and clapping her hands like Mae Marsh and Mary Pickford.

8. Sybil DelGaudio, *Dressing the Part: Sternberg, Dietrich, and Costume* (London: Associated University Presses, 1993), 132.

9. For a breakdown of the liberties in the film's costume design, see DelGaudio, *Dressing the Part*, 131–32.

10. See, for instance, Aristotle, *Rhetoric*, trans. J. H. Freese (Cambridge, MA: Harvard University Press, 1926), 1.13.13: "equity is justice that goes beyond the written law."

11. See the discussion of the blessings and dangers of the royal prerogative in John Locke, *Two Treatises of Government*, ed. Peter Laslett (Cambridge: Cambridge University Press, 1988), 377–78.

12. As Władysław Tatarkiewicz recounts it, the sixteenth-century Italian theory of visual arts already sought to acknowledge an irrationality to beauty, naming it after the "*non so che*" of Petrarch's sonnet "In nobil sangue vita umile et queta" (*Canzoniere* 215). See Władysław Tatarkiewicz, *History of Aesthetics III*, ed. D. Petsch (The Hague: Mouton, 1974), 201.

13. Charles Baudelaire, "Exposition Universelle (1855)" in id., *Œuvres Complètes*, eds. Claude Pichois and Jean Ziegler, vol. 2 (Paris: Gallimard, 1975–76), 578: "Le beau est toujours bizarre."

14. Kant, *Critique of the Power of Judgment*, 5: 229. Although Kant discusses human beauty in the following section, §17 "On the ideal of beauty," and asserts that the rational purpose immanent to a human being is a point of difference from free beauty, his pretense of finding in the average-sized man the empirical manifestation of this ideal (moral) beauty of the human person raises far more questions than it answers.

15. Cf. the link made between Hitler and the Bohemian tradition of Schwabing in northern Munich in Walter Benjamin, "The Work of Art in the Age of Its Technological Reproducibility: Second Version," trans. Edmund Jephcott and Harry Zohn in id., *The Work of Art in the Age of Its Technological Reproducibility and Other Writings on Media*, eds. Michael W. Jennings, Brigid Doherty, and Thomas Y. Levin (Cambridge, MA: Belknap Press of Harvard University Press, 2008), 41. The nineteenth-century tenet of the autonomy of art, by declaring that moral principles have no place in aesthetic appreciation, had lengthened nonconformism's line of credit, and rendered rule-following as such suspect. So long as the politicized bohemia of Hitler's cadre preserved some contact with the aesthetic domain, it could press a claim to indulgence for its adventurism because it could always protest that what it was undertaking was able to be properly judged—like the autonomous work of art of modernism—only by criteria immanent to it.

16. Cf. Marcel Oms, *Josef von Sternberg* (Paris: Anthologie du Cinéma, 1970), 541: "The triumph of the empress marks the defeat of the woman. At the end of this film, the Marlene

myth has reached the point of dehumanization." While these final scenes gesture toward cross-dressing, the resplendently white uniform with its fur trimmings and the rakishly-angled, towering mink papakha that Dietrich wears are not particularly committed to an erasure of femininity—they are hardly masculine attire. That one's humanity is somehow bound up with one's adherence to a gendered dress code is similarly assumed in Robin Wood, "*The Scarlet Empress*" in *International Dictionary of Films and Filmmakers - 1: Films*, eds. Tom Pendergast and Sara Pendergast (Detroit, MI: St. James Press, 2000), 1070: "Catherine herself, her natural desires frustrated and perverted, becomes the ultimate monster, cynically using her sexuality as a weapon. Her growing assumption of the male role is answered by the increasing feminization of her husband (at the climax, she is in soldier's uniform, he in a flowing white nightgown). The culmination is one of Hollywood's most ambiguous and devastating happy endings: the heroine triumphs over all adversity—at the expense of her humanity, and perhaps her sanity." Oms and Wood acknowledge in their panic what Kenneth Tynan had earlier famously praised in Dietrich. See Kenneth Tynan and Cecil Beaton, *Persona Grata* (London: Allan Wingate, 1953), 38: "She has sex, but no particular gender." The anxiety to which Oms and Wood admit in watching *The Scarlet Empress* is fortunately alien to the contemporaneous cycle of films starring Fred Astaire and Ginger Rogers, in which a shared impropriety of gender roles constitutes romance's condition of possibility. If their free-and-easy relationship to gender conventions compromises their grip on humanity—Astaire, with his large eyes, slight and swaying frame, and indomitable dancer's shoulders, at times resembles a praying mantis, while Rogers's extreme close-up from "We're in the Money" in *Gold Diggers of 1933* (1933), when she breaks into pig Latin and the camera zooms in and has to refocus, is a utopian encounter with a face beyond language, beyond all vanity and defensiveness—the price, in their judgment, is not prohibitive.

17. That the emergence of Dietrich as Dietrich has less to do with an intrusion of reality than with the "Real of cinema" is Badiou's contention in a comment on *Touch of Evil* (1958). See Alain Badiou, *Cinema*, trans. Susan Spitzer (Cambridge: Polity Press, 2013), 92: "I am thinking, for example, of the scene from Orson Welles' *Touch of Evil* in which the fat and crepuscular cop pays a visit to Marlene Dietrich. The local time is elicited here only because it really is Marlene Dietrich that Welles is visiting and because this idea does not at all coincide with the image, which should be that of a cop being entertained by an aging whore. The slow, almost ceremonial pace of the meeting derives from the fact that this apparent image must be traversed by thought up to the point at which, through an inversion of fictional values, we are dealing with Marlene Dietrich and Orson Welles, and not with a cop and a whore. The image is thereby wrested from itself so as to be restored to the Real of cinema."

18. At stake is not so much a substitution of Russia for Hollywood as a further foray into the indeterminable identity of Hollywood, for as John Ford remarked in a 1968 BBC interview with Philip Jenkinson: "Hollywood then or what is called, geographically called Hollywood, a place that none of us can define, we don't know where it is."

19. See George M. Wilson, *Seeing Fictions in Film: The Epistemology of Movies* (Oxford: Oxford University Press, 2011), 186: "When Alexey first arrives in Germany to meet Sophia, he surveys her appraisingly with a fatuously forceful look that parodies the gaze of the supposedly dominating male." For Wilson, Mulvey's account of Sternberg's work misses the comedy and the critique in such moments.

4 *THE DEVIL IS A WOMAN*: AGAINST THE OFF-SCREEN

1. On the earthliness of the idol as contradistinguished from the transcendence of the icon, see Marie-José Mondzain, *Image, Icon, Economy: The Byzantine Origins of the Contemporary Imaginary*, trans. Rico Franses (Stanford, CA: Stanford University Press, 2005).

2. A negative complement to this question would ask after the degree to which *The Devil Is a Woman* does not conform to the world-generating modes of production and reception analyzed in Daniel Yacavone, *Film Worlds: A Philosophical Aesthetics of Cinema* (New York: Columbia University Press, 2015). Drawing on Nelson Goodman and Hans-Georg Gadamer, Yacavone builds on the following thesis in Gilles Deleuze, *Cinema 2: The Time-Image*, trans. Hugh Tomlinson and Robert Galeta (London: Bloomsbury, 2013), 71: "The cinema does not just present images, it surrounds them with a world."

3. See George M. Wilson, *Narration in Light: Studies in Cinematic Point of View* (Baltimore, MD: Johns Hopkins University Press, 1986), 164: "The film image becomes a painterly field across which various encoded psychological forces are permitted visibly to play. [. . .] More generally, there exists a constant acknowledgement that what we are seeing is only a construction on film and is not to be simply taken as a transparent windowing onto a familiar, naturalistic world."

4. Carole Zucker, *The Idea of the Image: Josef von Sternberg's Dietrich Films*, 133. Following Zucker, one might consider Sternberg and Dietrich to be researching in their seven collaborations just where the breaking point lies at which the withholding of information from the viewer ceases to intrigue and induces instead indifference: that they should eventually have gone too far—in *The Devil Is a Woman*—was almost inevitable, given the empirical nature of the undertaking and the brinkmanship of those involved. By a nonetheless very different set of gestural means, Isabelle Huppert's performance in Michael Haneke's *The Piano Teacher* (2001) similarly explores the inverse correlation between psychological legibility and a viewer's engagement with a character. David Lynch's *Mulholland Drive* (2001) also goes too far, at least in terms of the genre of film noir, because its reticence in the imparting of elucidatory information is carried to the point where its images cease to subscribe to the noir tradition of invoking a larger, darker world of previously unsuspected corruption, indeed even calling into question instead whether the functional coherence of any world at all is what is to count as corrupt.

5. Charles Silver, *Marlene Dietrich* (New York: Pyramid, 1974), 65. See also Florence Jacobowitz, "Power and the Masquerade: *The Devil Is a Woman*," *Cineaction!* 8 (1987): 41: "Concha's appearance in the final sequence—her relaxed stance, softened makeup and less elaborate dress (the exact inverse of the introductory image) suggests succinctly that the strategies of masquerade and performance are necessitated by a social environment that distorts female identity into a perverse construct of 'femininity.'" For Jacobowitz, it is less important that we see Concha as she really is than that the grotesque stylizations of gender fall away once the gaze of the male characters Don Pasqual and Antonio no longer presides over her image. The film confronts the spectator with yet another incarnation of Concha "as she lingers contemplatively, deciding her next move. She is left on the road, alone, uncompromised and in transition."

6. This is, thankfully, not the ending that Joseph Breen, then head of the Production Code Administration, proposed in his correspondence with Paramount (*The Devil Is a Woman*, PCA file, Breen to Hammell, April 19, 1935). As though leading a man on were more offensive to morals than murder, Breen's suggestion was to alter the script so that Don Pasqual strangles Concha

when after the duel she comes to visit him in his hospital bed. Cited in Gaylyn Studlar, "Marlene Dietrich and the Erotics of Code-Bound Hollywood" in *Dietrich Icon*, eds. Gerd Gmünden and Mary R. Desjardins (Durham, NC: Duke University Press, 2007), 232.

7. Needless to say, the ordinary experience of channel surfing goes still further in the direction of the discontinuity of a sequence of images. The decreased semiotic coherence is counterbalanced, however, by the reassertion of the sensorimotor nexus in the act of selecting a new channel (although the viewer rarely expects to impose thereby a narrative order on the images, he or she can at least take comfort in a measure of control over all of them).

8. André Bazin, "Theater and Cinema" in id., *What is Cinema?*, trans. Hugh Gray, vol. 1 (Los Angeles: University of California Press, 2005), 104–5.

9. Noël Burch, *Theory of Film Practice*, trans. Helen R. Lane (London: Secker & Warburg, 1973), 64–65. The indistinctness of spaces in *The Blue Angel* is also touched on in Elisabeth Bronfen, *Heimweh: Illusionsspiele in Hollywood* (Berlin: Volk & Welt, 1999), 125.

10. Admittedly, the off-screen's associations with the profilmic were precisely what the editors of *Cahiers du Cinéma* came to dispute in the 1970s. Exemplary of this shift to give the term a metaphysical cast and to harness it for a Situationist polemic is Jean-Louis Comolli, *Cinema Against Spectacle: Technique and Ideology Revisited*, trans. Daniel Fairfax (Amsterdam: Amsterdam University Press, 2015), especially 134: "Against the spectacle, the cinema must show that the world is not totally visible, that seeing is seeing beyond the frame, seeing that there is an *hors-champ* which can not be framed. The *hors-champ* is not only what the frame hides by showing, it is everything that remains outside the possibility of being seen, outside the place of the spectator, it is what does not make the image (and thus what does not make the spectacle)." Here the off-screen (or *hors-champ*) is not simply the profilmic that could be filmed but happens to lie out of shot; it is the categorically unfilmable (the antifilmic rather than profilmic). For Eyal Peretz, the shot's contact with the off-screen prevents the image from closing in upon itself. See Eyal Peretz, *The Off-Screen: An Investigation of the Cinematic Frame* (Stanford, CA: Stanford University Press, 2017), 176: "The outside, or off-screen, functions as that which disconnects what we see on-screen from a clearly determinate order and context of things and thus prevents us from fully determining the meaningfulness of what we see. What we perceive on-screen thus forever maintains the status of a fragment, lacking fullness of context and therefore meaningfulness. Cinema is an art of shadows and ghosts because at the heart of the image is traced an indeterminate elsewhere that can never be actualized and that afflicts the image with an enigma or turns the image as such into an enigma." Yet the off-screen, in both the profilmic and antifilmic senses of the term, is a less than obvious choice for preventing the determination of meaning. Although the off-screen assigns the image the status of a fragment, it is disputable that in doing so it commits the image solely to a contestation of its meaningfulness. Reaction shots, for instance, acquire their legibility as such within a narrative through the practice of relating them to the profilmic off-screen. The antifilmic off-screen, since it is a feature of the frame of every shot, cannot be claimed to lay siege to the meaningfulness of a shot unless the visible component of the shot itself conspires with it against determinacy and context. In the case of *The Devil Is a Woman* I contend that spectacle gets by without the collusion of the off-screen in this task of holding the meaningfulness of a world at bay.

11. Sternberg, *Fun in a Chinese Laundry*, 267. See also Sternberg, "The Language of Film," *Image* 16, no. 2 (1973): 22–25. The text is a transcript of a tape monologue that Sternberg recorded in 1958. Declining to mention Lubitsch by name, he here places the responsibility for the change to the film's title on the "parasite who was usually in control of film production" (23).

12. Sternberg, *Fun in a Chinese Laundry*, 267.

13. Ibid., 268.

14. In the surviving fairground sequence from *The Case of Lena Smith*, Franz (James Hall) similarly bursts a woman's balloon to announce both his interest in her and the inauspicious nature of that interest.

15. See Mikhail Bakhtin, *Rabelais and His World*, trans. Hélène Iswolsky (Bloomington: Indiana University Press, 1984), 218. The epigraph for this chapter is also from this volume (7). Carnival, as Bakhtin investigates it, is an image without an off-screen: there are no spectators, only participants.

16. There is another such visual pun when Concha subsequently introduces Don Pasqual to her "mother" holding aloft the pet fish that he has just bought her, Concha declares: "Look, mama. I've got a fish."

17. Barbara Bowman, *Master Space: Film Images of Capra, Lubitsch, Sternberg, and Wyler* (New York: Greenwood Press, 1992), 105.

18. Bazin, "Theater and Cinema," 111.

19. Kendall L. Walton, *Mimesis as Make-Believe: On the Foundations of the Representational Arts* (Cambridge, MA: Harvard University Press, 1990).

20. Martin Heidegger, "The Origin of the Work of Art," trans. Julian Young in id., *Off the Beaten Track*, trans. Julian Young and Kenneth Haynes (Cambridge: Cambridge University Press, 2002), 22.

21. Ibid., 19.

22. See, for instance, the role of film in the standing reserve of technological civilization in Heidegger, "Insight Into That Which Is: Bremen Lectures 1949" in id., *Bremen and Freiburg Lectures*, trans. Andrew J. Mitchell (Bloomington: Indiana University Press, 2012), 36.

23. For a defense of the off-screen and its capacity to awaken thought, see Gregory Flaxman, "Out of Field: The Future of Film Studies," *Angelaki* 17, no. 4 (2012): 119–37. Referring to Stanley Kubrick's *2001: A Space Odyssey* (1968) to illustrate his notion of the off-screen (in which he is closer to Comolli than to Burch), Flaxman contrasts the film with what he deems the immersive spectacle of James Cameron's *Avatar* (2009). Yet inasmuch as he aligns the off-screen with the "irrational" cuts in *2001*, Flaxman distances his understanding of the term from the stitching together of images in a coherent world. The expansiveness that *2001* achieves is almost too large for any world—to secure it, to win for the individual images the freedom to float, the cuts have to be "irrational" so as to deny the off-screen its customary mediating function.

CONCLUSION: TOWARD AN ETHICS OF THE MOVING IMAGE

1. Cf. Paisley Livingston, "Theses on Cinema as Philosophy," *Journal of Aesthetics and Art Criticism* 64, no. 1 (January 2006): 11–18. Livingston argues that a dilemma attends the claim that a film contributes to philosophical debate by exclusively cinematic means: "If it is contended that the exclusively cinematic insight cannot be paraphrased, reasonable doubt arises with regard to its very existence. If it is granted, on the other hand, that the cinematic contribution can and must be paraphrased, this contention is incompatible with arguments for a significantly independent, innovative, and purely 'filmic' philosophical achievement, as linguistic mediation turns out to be constitutive of (our knowledge of) the epistemic contribution a film can make" (12). Yet given that paraphrase is defined by its relation to a source it does not exhaustively replicate and supplant, language can attest to cinema's specific contribution without becoming ensnared on Livingston's dilemma.

2. See Plato, *Republic*, 514a–515d and, for instance, *Romans* 1:22–24.

3. The star persona is an exception, albeit a very perverse one. Although the star persona is not restricted to the cinematic images in which the actor appears, the real life of this persona is not an affair of the flesh-and-blood individual who might be encountered in the street, at press interviews or elsewhere, instead finding itself truly at home only on the screen. Dietrich's public life was an interminable and herculean courtship of her screen image.

4. Emmanuel Levinas, *Ethics and Infinity: Conversations with Philippe Nemo*, trans. Richard A. Cohen (Pittsburgh, PA: Duquesne University Press, 1995), 86. The invisibility of the face is a corollary of the objecthood that is coextensive, for Levinas, with the visible (as though the gaze cannot relate to what is seen without reification). The face asserts itself in the ethical encounter without being seen, that is, objectified—it can be "seen" as a face only so long as it is not objectified in an image. The photographic likeness is, as it were, made to measure for illuminating what Levinas considers the offensiveness of images. The photographic likeness, inasmuch as it simply captures the appearance of that which is before the camera, does not lie and does not slander (admissible as evidence in a court of law, it is an ally in the quest to uncover the truth). And yet, even as it reliably reproduces the object before the camera, the image can cause offense to the sitter: its fault lies not in misrepresenting, but in the objectifying whereby it is able to represent at all. If photographic images cannot make good the truth deficit that, for Plato, characterizes all images presenting themselves to the senses, they nevertheless are readily credited, as unmanipulated records of the profilmic, with an automatic veracity that is not extended to the products of a painter or sculptor. This veracity, however, slips over into deceit and its own kind of caricature to the degree that the image is judged on its ability to show the person as person (and not as one more object in a world of objects).

5. Levinas, "Reality and Its Shadow" in id., *Collected Philosophical Essays*, trans. Alphonso Lingis (The Hague: Martinus Nijhoff, 1987), 1–14.

6. For a different assessment of the film's missed opportunity, see Don Willis, "Sternberg: The Context of Passion," *Sight and Sound* 47, no. 2 (Spring 1978): 106: "*The Shanghai Gesture* (1941) is a Sternberg image set without a film: namely, a virtuoso crane into the depths of a gambling pit near the beginning and a complementary crane out again at the end, echoed by more clipped tracks into the gamblers themselves. As an evocation of a human vortex of feeling and chance, this is as electric and concise a 'fix' on the Sternberg theme as there is. [. . .] Unfortunately, it's a case of editing and camerawork accomplishing in seconds what dull plot and duller talk fail to do in 90-plus minutes." See also Stéphane Benaïm, *Les visions d'Orient de Josef von Sternberg* (La Madeleine: Lettmotif, 2016), 122–23. Benaïm compares the geometry of vertigo of the film's opening with the geometry of imprisonment of the banquet scene.

7. We are confronted not so much with a face as with the fragment of time belonging to that face. See Noa Steimatsky, *The Face on Film* (Oxford: Oxford University Press, 2017), 71: "Certainly in von Sternberg's iconic shots of Dietrich one plainly sees how the facial image audaciously departs from narrative and discursive functions, to be enveloped with a silent-photographic quality, as if snatched not only from the narrative course of the film but from time altogether. Yet the swaying of plumes, furs, candles, reflections, shadows, and other micro-movements about Dietrich's face—all in addition to her marked voice—serve to amplify her very breathing, and with it a sense of living, embodied duration." With the act of recording, the camera provides the profilmic with access to the fountain of youth, although it is only the profilmic's cinematic simulacrum that can drink from it.

References

Aristotle. *Rhetoric*. Translated by J. H. Freese. Cambridge, MA: Harvard University Press, 1926.

Badiou, Alain. *Cinema*. Translated by Susan Spitzer. Cambridge: Polity Press, 2013.

Baeumler, Alfred. *Das Irrationalitätsproblem in der Ästhetik und Logik des 18. Jahrhunderts bis zur Kritik der Urteilskraft*. Darmstadt: Wissenschaftliche Buchgesellschaft, 1967.

Bakhtin, Mikhail. *Rabelais and His World*. Translated by Hélène Iswolsky. Bloomington: Indiana University Press, 1984.

Balázs, Béla. "Der sichtbare Mensch." In *Theory of the Film: Character and Growth of a New Art*. Translated by Edith Bone, 39–45. New York: Dover, 1970.

Baudelaire, Charles. "Exposition Universelle (1855)." In *Œuvres Complètes*. Edited by Claude Pichois and Jean Ziegler, 575–97. Vol. 2. Paris: Gallimard, 1975–76.

Baxter, Peter. "The Birth of Venus." *Wide Angle: A Film Quarterly of Theory, Criticism, and Practice* 10, no. 1 (1988): 4–15.

Baxter, Peter. *Just Watch!: Sternberg, Paramount and America*. London: British Film Institute, 1993.

Bazin, André. "Theater and Cinema." In *What is Cinema?* Translated by Hugh Gray, 76–124. Vol. 1. Los Angeles: University of California Press, 2005.

Bell, Allan. "Falling in Love Again and Again: Marlene Dietrich and the Iconization of Non-Native English." *Journal of Sociolinguistics* 15, no. 5 (November 1, 2011): 627–56.

Benaïm, Stéphane. *Les visions d'Orient de Josef von Sternberg*. La Madeleine: Lettmotif, 2016.

Benjamin, Walter. "The Work of Art in the Age of Its Technological Reproducibility: Second Version." Translated by Edmund Jephcott and Harry Zohn. In *The Work of Art in the Age of Its Technological Reproducibility and Other Writings on Media*. Edited by Michael W. Jennings, Brigid Doherty, and Thomas Y. Levin, 19–55. Cambridge, MA: Belknap Press of Harvard University Press, 2008.

Bloch, Ernst. *Traces*. Translated by Anthony A. Nassar. Stanford, CA: Stanford University Press, 2006.

Bogdanovich, Peter. *Who the Devil Made It*. New York: Ballantine, 1997.

Borges, Jorge Luis. "The Wall and the Books." Translated by James E. Irby. In *Labyrinths: Selected Stories and Other Writings*. Edited by James E. Irby and Donald A. Yates, 186–88. New York: New Directions, 1964.

Bovenschen, Silvia. "Is There a Feminine Aesthetic?" Translated by Beth Weckmueller. *New German Critique* 10 (Winter 1977): 111–37.

Bowman, Barbara. *Master Space: Film Images of Capra, Lubitsch, Sternberg, and Wyler*. New York: Greenwood Press, 1992.

Bronfen, Elisabeth. *Heimweh: Illusionsspiele in Hollywood*. Berlin: Volk & Welt, 1999.

Burch, Noël. *Theory of Film Practice*. Translated by Helen R. Lane. London: Secker & Warburg, 1973.

Cahiers du Cinéma editorial staff. "*Morocco*, de Josef von Sternberg." *Cahiers du Cinéma* 225 (November–December 1970): 5–13.

Cavell, Stanley. *Contesting Tears: The Hollywood Melodrama of the Unknown Woman*. Chicago: University of Chicago Press, 1996.

Comolli, Jean-Louis. *Cinema Against Spectacle: Technique and Ideology Revisited*. Translated by Daniel Fairfax. Amsterdam: Amsterdam University Press, 2015.

Conrad, Joseph. *The Nigger of the "Narcissus."* Oxford: Oxford University Press, 1984.

Constable, Catherine. *Thinking in Images: Film Theory, Feminist Philosophy and Marlene Dietrich*. London: BFI, 2005.

Deleuze, Gilles. *Cinema 1: The Movement-Image*. Translated by Hugh Tomlinson and Barbara Habberjam. London: Bloomsbury, 2013.

Deleuze, Gilles. *Cinema 2: The Time-Image*. Translated by Hugh Tomlinson and Robert Galeta. London: Bloomsbury, 2013.

DelGaudio, Sybil. *Dressing the Part: Sternberg, Dietrich, and Costume*. London: Associated University Presses, 1993.

Dietrich, Marlene. *My Life*. Translated by Salvator Attanasio. London: Weidenfeld and Nicolson, 1989.

Dirscherl, Luise and Gunther Nickel, eds. *Der Blaue Engel: Die Drehbuchentwürfe*. St. Ingbert: Röhrig, 2000.

Eisenstein, Sergei. "A Course in Treatment." In *Film Form: Essays in Film Theory*. Edited and translated by Jay Leyda, 84–107. London: Dennis Dobson, 1951.

Ekman, Paul, Wallace V. Friesen, and Phoebe Ellsworth. "What Are the Similarities and Differences in Facial Behavior across Cultures?" In *Emotion in the Human Face: Guidelines for Research and an Integration of Findings*, 153–67. New York: Pergamon, 1972.

Flaxman, Gregory. "Out of Field: The Future of Film Studies." *Angelaki* 17, no. 4 (2012): 119–37.

Flinn, Tom. "Joe, Where Are You? (Marlene Dietrich)." *Velvet Light Trap* 6 (Fall 1972): 17–20.

Furthman, Jules. Morocco *and* Shanghai Express: *Two Films by Josef von Sternberg*. New York: Simon and Schuster, 1973.

Grafe, Frieda. *Aus dem Off: Zum Kino in den Sechzigern*. Berlin: Brinkmann & Bose, 2003.

Haskell, Molly. *From Reverence to Rape: The Treatment of Women in the Movies*. New York: Holt, Rinehart and Winston, 1973.

Hegel, Georg Wilhelm Friedrich. *Aesthetics*. Translated by T. M. Knox. Oxford: Clarendon Press, 1975.

Heidegger, Martin. "Insight Into That Which Is: Bremen Lectures 1949." In *Bremen and Freiburg Lectures*. Translated by Andrew J. Mitchell, 3–73. Bloomington: Indiana University Press, 2012.

Heidegger, Martin. "The Origin of the Work of Art." In *Off the Beaten Track*. Translated by Julian Young and Kenneth Haynes, 1–56. Cambridge: Cambridge University Press, 2002.

Horwath, Alexander and Michael Omasta, eds. *Josef von Sternberg: The Case of Lena Smith*. Vienna: Synema, 2007.

Jacobowitz, Florence. "Power and the Masquerade: *The Devil Is a Woman*." *Cineaction!* 8 (1987): 32–41.

Jacobs, Lea. *The Wages of Sin: Censorship and the Fallen Woman Film 1928–1942*. Madison: University of Wisconsin Press, 1991.

Jelinek, Elfriede. "Das zweite Gesicht." *Die Zeit* (May 15, 1992): 75–76.

Jenkinson, Philip. "Von Sternberg's Last Interview." *Film Culture* 76 (1992): 40–43.

Kant, Immanuel. *Critique of the Power of Judgment*. Translated by Paul Guyer and Eric Matthews. Cambridge: Cambridge University Press, 2000.

Kant, Immanuel. *Critique of Pure Reason*. Translated by Norman Kemp Smith. London: Macmillan, 1929.

Kaplan, E. Ann. *Women and Film: Both Sides of the Camera*. New York: Methuen, 1983.

Kracauer, Siegfried. *From Caligari to Hitler: A Psychological History of the German Film*. Princeton, NJ: Princeton University Press, 1947.

Levinas, Emmanuel. *Ethics and Infinity: Conversations with Philippe Nemo*. Translated by Richard A. Cohen. Pittsburgh, PA: Duquesne University Press, 1995.

Levinas, Emmanuel. "Reality and Its Shadow." In *Collected Philosophical Essays*. Translated by Alphonso Lingis, 1–14. The Hague: Martinus Nijhoff, 1987.

Livingston, Paisley. "Theses on Cinema as Philosophy." *Journal of Aesthetics and Art Criticism* 64, no. 1 (January 2006): 11–18.

Locke, John. *Two Treatises of Government*. Edited by Peter Laslett. Cambridge: Cambridge University Press, 1988.

Marchetti, Gina. *Romance and the "Yellow Peril": Race, Sex, and Discursive Strategies in Hollywood Fiction*. Berkeley: University of California Press, 1993.

Mérigeau, Pascal. *Josef von Sternberg*. Paris: Edilig, 1983.

Mitry, Jean. *The Aesthetics and Psychology of the Cinema*. Translated by Christopher King. Bloomington: Indiana University Press, 1997.

Modleski, Tania. *Feminism Without Women: Culture and Criticism in a "Postfeminist" Age*. Abingdon: Routledge, 1991.

Mondzain, Marie-José. *Image, Icon, Economy: The Byzantine Origins of the Contemporary Imaginary*. Translated by Rico Franses. Stanford, CA: Stanford University Press, 2005.

Mulvey, Laura. *Visual and Other Pleasures*. New York: Palgrave, 1989.

Nancy, Jean-Luc. *Philosophical Chronicles*. Translated by Franson Manjali. New York: Fordham University Press, 2008.

Naremore, James. *Acting in the Cinema*. Berkeley: University of California Press, 1988.

Ngai, Sianne. "Black Venus, *Blonde Venus*." In *Bad Modernisms*. Edited by Douglas Mao and Rebecca L. Walkowitz, 145–78. Durham, NC: Duke University Press, 2006.

Nichols, Bill. *Ideology and the Image*. Bloomington: Indiana University Press, 1981.

Oms, Marcel. *Josef von Sternberg*. Paris: Anthologie du Cinéma, 1970.

Peretz, Eyal. *The Off-Screen: An Investigation of the Cinematic Frame*. Stanford, CA: Stanford University Press, 2017.

Proust, Marcel. *The Guermantes Way*. Translated by Mark Treharne. London: Penguin, 2002.

Riva, Maria. *Marlene Dietrich: By Her Daughter*. London: Bloomsbury, 1992.

Sarris, Andrew. *The Films of Josef von Sternberg*. New York: The Museum of Modern Art, 1966.

Shakespeare, William. *Antony and Cleopatra*. Edited by John Wilders. Arden Third Series. London: Bloomsbury, 1995.

Silver, Charles. *Marlene Dietrich*. New York: Pyramid, 1974.

Smith, Jack. "Belated Appreciation of V. S." *Film Culture* 31 (1963–64): 4–5.

Steimatsky, Noa. *The Face on Film*. Oxford: Oxford University Press, 2017.

von Sternberg, Josef. *Fun in a Chinese Laundry*. London: Secker & Warburg, 1966.

von Sternberg, Josef. "The Language of Film." *Image* 16, no. 2 (1973): 22–25.

Studlar, Gaylyn. "Marlene Dietrich and the Erotics of Code-Bound Hollywood." In *Dietrich Icon*. Edited by Gerd Gmünden and Mary R. Desjardins, 211–38. Durham, NC: Duke University Press, 2007.

Studlar, Gaylyn. *In the Realm of Pleasure: Von Sternberg, Dietrich, and the Masochistic Aesthetic*. New York: Columbia University Press, 1988.

Tatarkiewicz, Władysław. *History of Aesthetics III*. Edited by D. Petsch. The Hague: Mouton, 1974.

Tawa, Michael. *Agencies of the Frame: Tectonic Strategies in Cinema and Architecture*. Newcastle upon Tyne: Cambridge Scholars, 2011.

Tynan, Kenneth and Cecil Beaton. *Persona Grata*. London: Allan Wingate, 1953.

Walton, Kendall L. *Mimesis as Make-Believe: On the Foundations of the Representational Arts*. Cambridge, MA: Harvard University Press, 1990.

Weinberg, Herman G. *Josef von Sternberg: A Critical Study*. New York: E. P. Dutton, 1967.

Weiss, Andrea. *Vampires and Violets: Lesbians in Film*. London: Cape, 1992.

Willis, Don. "Sternberg: The Context of Passion." *Sight and Sound* 47, no. 2 (Spring 1978): 104–9.

Wilson, George M. *Narration in Light: Studies in Cinematic Point of View*. Baltimore, MD: Johns Hopkins University Press, 1986.

Wilson, George M. *Seeing Fictions in Film: The Epistemology of Movies*. Oxford: Oxford University Press, 2011.

Wollen, Peter. *Signs and Meaning in the Cinema*. London: British Film Institute, 1998.

Wood, Robin. "*The Scarlet Empress*." In *International Dictionary of Films and Filmmakers - 1: Films*. Edited by Tom Pendergast and Sara Pendergast, 1069–70. Detroit, MI: St. James Press, 2000.

Wood, Robin. "Venus de Marlene." *Film Comment* 14, no. 2 (March–April 1978): 58–63.

Yacavone, Daniel. *Film Worlds: A Philosophical Aesthetics of Cinema*. New York: Columbia University Press, 2015.

Zucker, Carole. *The Idea of the Image: Josef von Sternberg's Dietrich Films*. Cranbury, NJ: Associated University Press, 1988.

Index

Abrahamic religions, 94–97
Alvarado, Don, 102
American Tragedy, An (Sternberg), 19–21
Angel (Lubitsch), 57
appearance, 4, 14, 17, 19–21, 52–53, 58–59, 84, 96, 100
   and beauty, 46, 64, 73
   and truth, 16, 23–28, 30–40, 45, 50, 69
Aristotle, 64
Arnold, Edward, 102
Astaire, Fred, 112n16
Atwill, Lionel, 75, 77
audience, 7–10, 28–30, 33, 36–38, 47–55, 61–62, 64, 67, 76
   See also direct audience address
autonomy, 4, 6, 13, 19–20, 74, 106n10, 111n15
Avatar (Cameron), 115n23

Badiou, Alain, 112n17
Baeumler, Alfred, 40
Baker, Josephine, 49
Bakhtin, Mikhail, 115n15
Balázs, Béla, 2–3
Ballbusch, Peter, 63
Bancroft, George, 49
Banton, Travis, 29

battle of the sexes, 15, 69
Baudelaire, Charles, 65
Baudrillard, Jean, 94
Baxter, Peter, 51, 110n13, 110n16, 110n1
Bazin, André, 12, 79, 87
Bell, Allan, 105n6
Belle Hélène, La (Offenbach), 44
Benaïm, Stéphane, 116n6
Benjamin, Walter, 111n15
Berkeley, Busby, 32
Bildungsroman, 70
Bizet, Georges, 84
Bloch, Ernst, 50
Blonde Venus (Sternberg), 16, 19, 41–58
"Blonde Women" (Holländer), 51
Blue Angel, The (Sternberg), 2, 20, 46, 49, 51, 79–80, 106n8
Borges, Jorge Luis, 50
Bouhours, Dominique, 40, 65
bourgeois marriage, 36
Bovenschen, Silvia, 53–54
Bowman, Barbara, 87
Breen, Joseph, 113n6
Brejchová, Jana, 17
Brent, Evelyn, 3, 49
Brook, Clive, 24, 49
Burch, Noël, 79–80, 115n23

Cagney, James, 32
California, 18, 23
Cameron, James, 115n23
camp, 59, 108n13
Capriccio Espagnol (Rimsky-Korsakov), 82
Carmen (Mérimée), 89
carnival, 82–85, 89
Carstensen, Margit, 6
Case of Lena Smith, The (Sternberg), 110n16, 115n14
Cavell, Stanley, 109n2
Channing, Carol, 105n6
Chaplin, Charlie, 2, 60
Chautard, Émile, 30
China, 23, 28, 30, 32
Christie, Agatha, 23
Clark, Davison, 72
close-up, 1, 3–4, 9, 11, 39–40, 68, 83–84, 96, 98–99, 112n16
Closser Hale, Louise, 29
Colton, John, 97
Columbia Pictures, 15, 83, 108n13
Comolli, Jean-Louis, 114n10, 115n23
Compson, Betty, 3, 100
computer games, 14
Conrad, Joseph, 60
Constable, Catherine, 108n21
continuity, 13, 38–39, 78
Cooper, Gary, 4, 8, 10
Coslow, Sam, 49
costume drama, 59–62, 64, 67
Crime and Punishment (Sternberg), 15, 102

Dames (Enright and Berkeley), 108n14
Daumier, Honoré, 86
Debord, Guy, 94, 97
Dee, Frances, 20
Deleuze, Gilles, 39, 113n2
DelGaudio, Sybil, 62
despotism, 59–60, 63–65, 67, 69, 74
Destry Rides Again (Marshall), 16, 21
The Devil Is a Woman (Sternberg), 19, 23, 34, 64, 75–79, 81–89, 96, 110n3
Dietrich, Marlene
  and accent, 7
  and beauty, 2–4, 11, 27, 33, 37, 44, 46, 58, 64–65, 67
  as collaborator, 4, 10, 16, 20–21, 45, 102
  as comic, 49, 62, 67, 89
  and cross-dressing, 8–9, 70
  and discipline, 5, 54
  and emotional inscrutability, 2, 39, 77

  as singer, 7–8, 16, 46–52
  as star, 1, 3–4, 10, 15–16, 19, 34, 45, 49–50, 52, 56, 60, 62, 70, 85, 96, 116n3
  See also by film titles
direct audience address, 98–99
Dishonored (Sternberg), 19
Docks of New York, The (Sternberg), 100
documentary, 70, 82, 92–93, 102
Dos Passos, John, 76
Dreiser, Theodore, 19
Dresser, Louise, 63, 65
Dreyer, Carl, 106n11
Dubin, Al, 108n14

Eagle, The (Brown), 65
Eisenstein, Sergei, 21, 72
ethics, 3–4, 12–13, 16–17, 26, 60, 64, 91–93, 96–98, 100
Evening with Marlene Dietrich, An (Jones), 53
evil, 97–99
eyeline matches, 78, 84

faith, 24–27, 35–40
Falconetti, Renée Jeanne, 106n11
fame, 3, 4, 7, 34
farce, 61–63, 65, 74
Fassbinder, Rainer Werner, 6–7
feminist film criticism, 12
Femme et le Pantin, La (Louÿs), 76
femme fatale, 19–20, 77
fetish, 93, 106n10
fiction, 12, 35–37, 40, 42, 70, 76, 81, 88, 95–96, 99–103
fictional character, 37, 93, 96, 100, 103
Flaxman, Gregory, 115n23
Follow Thru (Corrigan and Schwab), 49
Footlight Parade (Bacon and Berkeley), 32
Ford, John, 31, 112n18
forgiveness, 36, 57
fourth wall, 99
Fox Film Corporation, 107n11
Franco, Francisco, 82
Freud, Sigmund, 101
Furthman, Jules, 23, 27, 29, 37, 39, 41, 69, 110n16

Garbo, Greta, 1, 6, 60, 70
Garmes, Lee, 2, 109n1
gaze, 1, 4, 10–14, 41, 53–54, 87, 103, 108n16, 112n19, 113n5, 116n4
Gentlemen Prefer Blondes (Hawks), 25, 28
gesture, 2–3, 5, 9, 53, 72, 102, 113n4
glamor, 21, 33, 63, 101, 107n4
Glennon, Bert, 64, 109n1

Gogh, Vincent van, 14
Gold Diggers of 1933 (LeRoy and Berkeley), 112n16
Golding, William, 101
Gone with the Wind (Fleming), 107n13
Grabbe, Christian, 63
grace, 65
Grant, Cary, 41, 51, 56, 109n2
Grant, Lawrence, 24
Grease (Kleiser), 62
Great Dictator, The (Chaplin), 60
Griffith, David Wark, 78

Hale, Georgia, 3
Hall, James, 115n14
Haneke, Michael, 113n4
happy ending, 36, 42, 112n16
Haskell, Molly, 57
Hawks, Howard, 25
Hegel, Georg Wilhelm Friedrich, 11, 105n5
Heidegger, Martin, 88
Hermann, Irm, 6–7
Hervey, Harry, 23
Hitchcock, Alfred, 26, 56, 82
Hitler, Adolf, 111n15
Hobbes, Thomas, 67
Holmes, Phillips, 19, 21
horror movie, 108n16
"Hot Voodoo" (Coslow and Rainger), 46, 48–52, 54–56
Hughes, Howard, 69
Hunte, Otto, 80
Huppert, Isabelle, 113n4

I Am a Fugitive from a Chain Gang (LeRoy), 58
I, Claudius (Sternberg), 19
"I Couldn't Be Annoyed" (Robin and Whiting), 52
iconoclasm, 93–96
idolatry, 4, 75, 93, 96–97
irony, 48, 53–54, 69, 106n15, 108n16, 109n4
Ivan the Terrible (Eisenstein), 72

Jacobowitz, Florence, 113n5
Jacobs, Lea, 57
Jaffe, Sam, 66
Jannings, Emil, 19, 20, 50, 106n8
Jelinek, Elfriede, 53
Jet Pilot (Sternberg et al.), 69
justice, 60, 64–65

Kafka, Franz, 7
Kahn, Madeline, 106n6

Kant, Immanuel, 27, 65
Kaplan, E. Ann, 105n5
Keeler, Ruby, 32
King Kong (Cooper and Schoedsack), 51
kitsch, 84, 108n13
Kleiser, Randal, 62
knowledge, 25, 27, 36–37, 40, 70, 77
Komroff, Manuel, 61
Kubrick, Stanley, 115n23

La Roy, Rita, 47
Last Command, The (Sternberg), 19, 50
Laughton, Charles, 19
Lauren, S. K., 41
Leibniz, Gottfried Wilhelm, 40, 65
Leigh, Janet, 69
LeRoy, Mervyn, 58
Levinas, Emmanuel, 96–97, 107n1
likeness, 91–93, 101
Livingston, Paisley, 115n1
Locke, John, 64
Lodge, John, 67, 83
Lord of the Flies (Golding), 101
Lorre, Peter, 102
Louÿs, Pierre, 76
Lubitsch, Ernst, 57, 68, 82
Luke, Keye, 98
Lynch, David, 113n4

make-believe, 23, 35–37, 40, 45, 88, 100
Mamoulian, Rouben, 60
Manet, Édouard
Marchetti, Gina, 31
Marshall, George, 16
Marshall, Herbert, 41, 57, 109n2
Marx Brothers, 63
Méliès, Georges, 96
Menjou, Adolphe, 8
Mérigeau, Pascal, 107n18
Mérimée, Prosper, 84
messianism, 50, 88
Meyer, Russ, 69
Meyerhold, Vsevolod, 72
Millandy, Georges, 7
Mitry, Jean, 13
Mizoguchi, Kenji, 71
Modleski, Tania, 109n4
monarchy, 60, 64–65
Monroe, Marilyn, 25–26
Moore, Dickie, 41–42
Morgan, Gene, 44
Morocco (Sternberg), 4, 7–10, 14, 49

Motion Picture Producers and Distributors of America (MPPDA), 56–57
Mulholland Drive (Lynch), 113n4
Mulvey, Laura, 10–11, 33, 112n19
Muni, Paul, 58
Munson, Ona, 97, 107n13
Murnau, Friedrich Wilhelm, 20
Muse, Clarence, 48
musicals, 62
myth, 44–45, 52–55, 58, 67, 70, 111–112n16

Nana (Zola), 44–45
Nancy, Jean-Luc, 24
Naremore, James, 15–16
narrative, 15–19, 38, 75–76, 81
Nestroy, Johann, 63
Ngai, Sianne, 49
Night Café, The (van Gogh), 14
Novak, Kim, 26

objectification, 1, 11–14, 46, 96, 99, 101, 116n4
Offenbach, Jacques, 44
off-screen, 75–76, 78–79, 81–82, 84, 87–88
Oland, Warner, 24, 107n11
Oms, Marcel, 111–112n16
O'Neal, Zelma, 49
Ornitz, Samuel, 110n16
Ozu, Yasujiro, 10

painting, 14, 79, 81, 86, 91–93, 95
Pallette, Eugene, 30
Paramount, 5, 10, 15, 21, 23, 29, 35, 49, 63, 67, 70, 103, 113n6
  management of, 19, 44, 57, 59, 60, 68, 83
  publicity machine of, 2, 47, 52
Patriot, The (Lubitsch), 68
Paul, 25–26
perception, 4, 9, 12–17, 38–39, 51, 58, 78–79, 92
Peretz, Eyal, 114n10
Petrarch, 111n12
Piano Teacher, The (Haneke), 113n4
Platonism, 60, 94–95, 97
Porcasi, Paul, 8
prerogative
  head of state's, 59, 65, 67
  husband's, 42
  performer's, 10
  spectator's, 52
Production Code, 29, 113n6
profilmic, 18, 33, 54, 81–82, 87, 91–96, 98–100, 102–103, 108n16
propaganda, 76

prostitution, 28–30, 32–33, 38, 42, 45, 55, 63
Proust, Marcel, 108n21
psychoanalysis, 14

"Quand l'amour meurt" (Crémieux and Millandy), 7–8, 10
Queen Christina (Mamoulian), 60, 70

Rainger, Ralph, 48, 89
realism, 10, 12, 23, 32, 45, 62, 81, 87–88, 101
Rimsky-Korsakov, Nikolai, 82
Riva, Maria, 61, 110n10, 111n6
RKO, 83
Robin, Leo, 89
Rogers, Ginger, 112n16
Romero, Cesar, 75, 77
Roosevelt, Franklin Delano, 32
Russia, 50, 60, 63, 68–70

Saga of Anatahan, The (Sternberg), 83, 101
Sarris, Andrew, 56
Scarlet Empress, The (Sternberg), 19, 23, 59–74, 83
Schubert, Franz, 109n5
Schygulla, Hanna, 6
sculpture, 18, 63, 91–93, 95
Semon, Larry, 102
sensorimotor nexus, 11–14, 16
Seyffertitz, Gustav von, 30
Shanghai Express (Sternberg), 19, 23–41, 43–45, 63
Shanghai Gesture, The (Sternberg), 97–99, 107–108n13
show business, 44, 46, 50, 55, 58
Sidney, Sylvia, 20
silent film, 1–3
Silver, Charles, 77
Smith, Jack, 15
Society of the Spectacle, The (Debord), 97
Song of Songs, The (Mamoulian), 60
sound film, 1–3, 6, 81
space, 37, 39–40, 50–51, 87–88, 92
  and viewer, 9–14, 75, 78–81, 84, 97, 99–100
Spain, 82–85
spectacle, 21, 23, 24, 26–27, 37–38, 44, 50, 55, 59, 76, 84
  and beauty, 46, 58
  and cinema, 4, 12–13, 16–19, 33, 88, 93–94, 103, 114n10, 115n23
Stagecoach (Ford), 31
Stage Fright (Hitchcock), 82
Steimatsky, Noa, 116n7

Sternberg, Josef von
  on actors, 4–5
  and agression toward Dietrich, 34, 84
  and cinematic philosophy, 17
  and identification with Dietrich, 5, 14–15
  and on-screen proxies, 15
  and studio shoots, 17, 23, 60, 101–102
  See also by film titles
Stevens, Ruthelma, 66
Stewart, James, 16, 26
Sunrise (Murnau), 20

Tatarkiewicz, Władysław, 111n12
Tawa, Michael, 106n11
Tell, Olive, 61
theater, 3, 11, 13, 43–46, 50, 55, 79,
  99–100
Third-Class Carriage, The (Daumier), 86
"Three Sweethearts Have I" (Rainger and
  Robin), 89
Tierney, Gene, 97–99
Touch of Evil (Welles), 112n17
truth, 60, 65, 76–77, 82, 88, 92, 94–95
  See also appearance and truth
2001: A Space Odyssey (Kubrick), 115n23
Tynan, Kenneth, 112n16

Underworld (Sternberg), 49, 102, 109n1
unreliable narrator, 75, 82

Valentino, Rudolph, 65
van Gogh, Vincent. *See* Gogh, Vincent van
Vertigo (Hitchcock), 26
virtual reality, 14

Walton, Kendall L., 88
Warren, Harry, 108n14
Wayne, John, 69
Weiss, Andrea, 106n9
Welles, Orson, 112n17
West, Mae, 67
Willis, Don, 116n6
Wilson, George M., 112n19, 113n3
Wollen, Peter, 107n4
Wong, Anna May, 23, 30
Wood, Robin, 109n3, 112n16
world, 20–21, 26, 32, 36–37, 40, 43, 45, 50, 63,
  69, 99, 109n2, 110n16
  and images, 12, 16–18, 73, 75–76, 78–82,
  87–89, 95, 103, 113n4
Wray, Fay, 51

Yacavone, Daniel, 113n2
"You Little So-And-So" (Coslow and
  Robin), 52

Zola, Émile, 44–45
Zucker, Carole, 77–78, 106n7, 111n7
Zukor, Adolph, 60